Play Jazz · Blues · 1

PIANO BY EAR

BOOK ONE

Online Audio

by ANDY OSTWALD

www.melbay.com/98565MEB

CD contents

Cover photo and design by the author
All music created and performed by the author

3 4 5 6 7 8 9 0

Visit us on the Web at www.melbay.com — E-mail us at email@melbay.com

PRAISE FOR PIANO BY EAR

Piano by Ear is a refreshingly innovative approach to jazz, blues, and rock piano. It effectively introduces improvising, ear training, and music theory, and features beautifully performed and recorded musical examples. I recommend *Piano by Ear* for self-study as well as for private and group instruction.

—Dee Spencer
Co-director, Jazz and World Music Studies program at S.F. State University
Executive Board Member, International Association of Jazz Educators

Piano by Ear is a welcome, modern, and original approach to ear training literature. It is a user-friendly, wisely written book series, and I highly recommend it.

—Mark Levine
author of "The Jazz Piano Book" and "The Jazz Theory Book"

Piano by Ear lays out clearly, for the first time in my memory, a method for developing the art of playing by ear as it relates to playing jazz, rock, and the blues. What's more, the recorded improvisations are of very high quality, both in technical realization and beauty—they are true piano playing and should prove both motivational and inspirational.

—Ken Durling
retailer of music method books and sheet music
composer

There is no doubt that *Piano by Ear* is the work of an experienced and effective teacher. The organization of the books, the clarity of the explanations, and the absolutely wonderful "Practicing Pages" demonstrate mature pedagogy. Thanks to the recorded examples, even teachers with little or no jazz/blues/rock experience can teach the approach successfully. *Piano by Ear* is definitely going on this reviewer's jazz piano workshop "Recommended Materials" list. (From a review in the *American Music Teacher* journal.)

—Ann Collins
professor emeritus of Jazz Studies, Western Illinois University
author of "Jazz Works"
co-author of the MTNA/IAJE Jazz Studies Guide

CONTENTS

ACKNOWLEDGEMENTS

Thanks to Bill Bay and the staff at Mel Bay Publications for their guidance from start to finish; to editors Wendy Weiner and John Raeside for their many contributions to the conversational tone and clarity of the text; to Jen Serota for the production work on the *Piano by Ear* cover design; to Shawn Hazen for his help with the layout of the books; and to John Ewing and David Bergen for answering all of my computer questions. I also want to thank Peck Allmond, Bill Freais, Ben Goldberg, Bridget Laky, Mark Levine, Robin Linnett, John McArdle, David Motto, Kenneth Nash, Steve Ostwald, Jenn Shreve, and Andrea Silvestri for their valuable contributions and insights.

Special thanks to Bud Spangler of *Syntropy Audio* for the loan of his great recording equipment and for his advice on microphone placement; to Dave Bell of *Bell Boy Recording* for mixing the CDs; and to Hans Christian of *Allemande Music* for mastering them.

Thanks also to the many students who have studied unpublished versions of *Piano by Ear* as their enthusiasm, questions, and musical development have been my guide and inspiration. Finally, thanks to my family and friends for their encouragement. *Piano by Ear* is dedicated to the memory of my dad, Kurt Ostwald.

ABOUT THE AUTHOR

Photo by Steve Ostwald

Jazz pianist, Andy Ostwald, performs in the San Francisco area and now-and-again on tour in the States and abroad. A teacher of jazz, blues, and rock piano for twenty years, he has also worked as an ensemble coach for the *Berkeley Jazz Workshop, Oaktown Jazz Workshops,* and the *Feather River Youth Jazz Camp,* and has conducted *Music for Dancers* workshops at the University of Santa Clara. Ostwald studied with jazz pianist Harold Mabern, classical pianist Sylvia Jenkins, and composer Lou Harrison. For more information about the author, please visit his website:

www.andyostwald.com

INTRODUCTION

Welcome to *Piano by Ear!* This comprehensive introduction to jazz, blues, and rock piano will offer easy-to-understand explanations of relevant music theory, and guide you step by step as you develop your skills. Above all, *Piano by Ear* will help you to explore and develop your ability to improvise. Rather than focus on written notation, you'll learn to express yourself at the piano by relying on your *ear* and on your own creative instincts.

BOOK ONE

Book One of *Piano by Ear* is designed for those who are brand-new to playing music by ear and improvising. It's also great for those who already have some experience, but want to strengthen their grasp of the basics.

As for piano technique, you need just enough to play chords with your left hand and single notes with your right hand (nothing too fast). You'll also need a rudimentary knowledge of treble and bass clef so that you can read the written examples.

STUDYING BY EAR AND IMPROVISING GO HAND IN HAND

To gain the skill and understanding that lies at the heart of improvising, musicians study music by ear. This is how they learn to work with music based on how it sounds rather than how it looks on paper. It's also how they acquire a true feeling for the nuances and spirit of a given musical style.

There are numerous books on improvising that advocate learning by ear. The unique contribution of *Piano by Ear* is to show you how it's done. Complete with guidelines and recorded examples that demystify the practice, this book/CD series begins very simply, builds gradually, and ultimately helps prepare you for learning directly from the recordings of your favorite artists.

LEARN BY DOING

Along with learning by ear, improvising is something you learn by *doing. Piano by Ear* will serve as your guide as you progress from playing "two-chord jams" to full-blown jazz, rock, and blues improvisations. Each chapter will feature a new improvisation.

Music Theory

Music theory is only introduced as it becomes relevant to the music you're playing. This approach will guard against *information overload* and help you fully integrate what you're learning.

Improvising Techniques

Like a good story, a compelling improvisation includes twists and turns, while maintaining a sense of continuity. *Piano by Ear* will show you a number of the techniques musicians use to create these improvisations, and guide you as you explore them in your own improvisations.

Composing

Piano by Ear will encourage you to do a little composing. Specifically, it will suggest that you make up and write down melodic phrases that you can then weave into your improvisations. This practice is invaluable—it gives you a way to develop musical ideas apart from the moment-to-moment concerns of improvising. (Previous experience with composing is not necessary.)

The Accompanying CD

The improvisations recorded on the accompanying CD are intended to be a source of inspiration as well as a means of instruction. They were created with the idea that uncomplicated music—even music that is simple enough to introduce the practice of learning by ear—can spark the imagination and be a joy to listen to.

A Proven Method

I have used *Piano by Ear* with my students for years with exciting results. The youngest student was twelve, the oldest, about sixty. Some studied with the ambition of developing a professional career. Others played solely for their own enjoyment. Hearing the feedback and watching the creative development of these students served as my guide and inspiration in revising, expanding, and fine-tuning the series for this publication.

Equipment

- a piano or keyboard
- a CD player that can be set up at your piano (a portable player is fine)
- a pair of headphones

Chapter One

C MAJOR

It seems, then, to be one of the paradoxes of creativity that in order to think originally, we must familiarize ourselves with the ideas of others.

—George Kneller
from "The Art and Science of Creativity"

NOTES OF THE SCALE

The music in Chapter One will be in the key of C major and created entirely from the notes of the
C major scale:

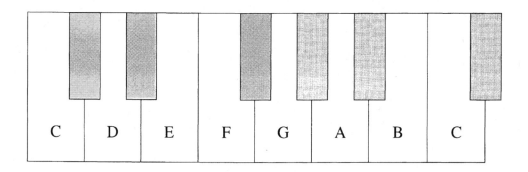

CHOOSE THE NOTES AS YOU PLAY

Using your right hand, play the notes of the C major scale *out of order*. You might, for example,
begin on the note, B, then jump down to D, return to B, move on to A, and so on. Just choose
the notes as you play. Create different rhythms by holding the notes for different lengths of time
—long notes, short notes, and anything in between:

Some of your note sequences may have an abstract, freeform quality, while others may sound
like the melody to a song. Either way is okay. There are no wrong answers here!

*Give this exercise a whirl before you read on—immerse yourself in the sounds you are creating
and play for a minute or two.*

IMPROVISING RHYTHM

When you improvise, the rhythms you create are just as important as the notes you choose to play. The *Improvising Rhythm* exercises offered throughout Book One will help you to develop your rhythm skills. This chapter's exercise features a four-beat count:

1. Begin by counting slowly and steadily as follows: "1 ~ 2 ~ 3 ~ 4 ~ 1 ~ 2 ~ 3 ~ 4 ~ 1..." You can count aloud or to yourself—the important thing is that you remain fully aware of the counts.

2. Continue counting slowly and steadily and—using your right hand only—play a note every time you say "1." Hold each note until you play the next note. Use notes from the C major scale. Focus on *when* you play a note—*which* note you play is of secondary importance in this exercise:

3. Once you can comfortably play a note on each "1," switch to playing on each "2"; remember to hold each note until you play the next note. Once you can comfortably play on each "2," switch to playing on each "3"; then, on each "4." *This exercise can be challenging—please be patient:* [1]

4. *(You may want to save steps 4 and 5 for subsequent practice sessions.)* Vary the beat on which you play a note. For example, you might play a note on "3" in your first measure, on "1" in your second measure, on "4" in the next measure, etc. As before, hold each note until you play the next note:

5. Now, explore playing one note, two notes, three notes, four notes, or even *no* notes in a given measure. For example, you might play on "1" and "4" in your first measure, on none of the beats in your second measure, on "2," "3," and "4" in your third measure, and so on. *You can create numerous rhythms this way; experiment with the different possibilities as you play.* Remember to remain fully aware of the counts and to hold each note until you play the next note.

 An example of step 5 is offered on Track 1 of the accompanying CD. Set up your CD player so that you can use it while sitting at your piano. Then, listen to the example—the first few measures are written below so that you can follow along as you listen.[2] (Remember that Track 1 is just an example; the notes and rhythms that you play will be up to you.)

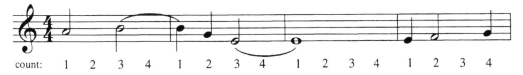

count: 1   2   3   4   1   2   3   4   1   2   3   4   1   2   3   4

[1] Did you know? A curved line drawn between two notes of the same pitch is a *tie*. The second note of a tie is held over from the first note rather than played.

[2] In case you need a refresher course on time signatures, the top number tells you how many beats there are in a measure and the bottom number tells you the rhythmic value of each beat. 4/4 indicates that there are four beats in a measure and that each beat is equivalent to a quarter note.

BUILDING CHORDS

The upcoming improvisation will include chords derived from the C major scale. To build these chords, number the notes of the C major scale 1 through 7. The notes appear here in bass clef:

Each note can be used as the foundation, or *root,* of a chord. *1* is the root of the "one chord," which is written with the Roman numeral **I**. *2* is the root of the "two chord," which is written with the Roman numeral **II**, and so on.

TRIADS

Triads are three-note chords. To build a triad, stack three alternate notes of the scale starting with the root of the chord:

Build the **I** triad by stacking three alternate notes of the scale starting on *1:*

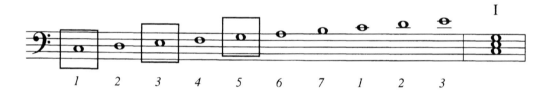

Build the **II** triad by stacking three alternate notes of the scale starting on *2:*

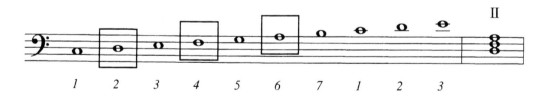

Build triads **I** through **VII**. Check your work below:

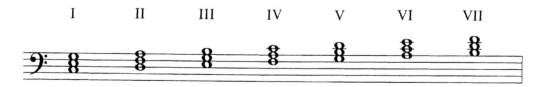

SEVENTH CHORDS

Seventh chords are four-note chords. To build a seventh chord, stack four alternate notes of the scale starting with the root of the chord:

Build the **I** seventh chord by stacking four alternate notes of the scale starting on *1:*

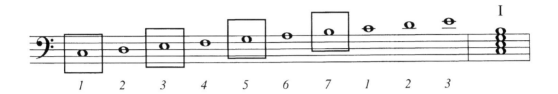

Build the **II** seventh chord by stacking four alternate notes of the scale starting on *2:*

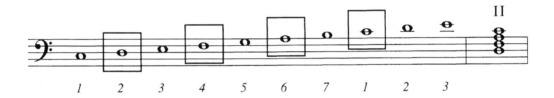

Build seventh chords **I** through **VII**. Check your work below:

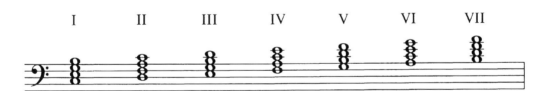

> Seventh chords get their name from the fact that they span seven letter names from their root up to their top note. The **III** seventh chord, for example, spans seven letter names from E up to D:
>
> E — F — G — A — B — C — D

The complete names of the triads and seventh chords you've just built are shown below. The symbols that follow the Roman numerals will be explained in Book Two.[1] For now, just note that the seventh chords include a "7" in their name, making it easy to distinguish seventh chords from triads.

Triads

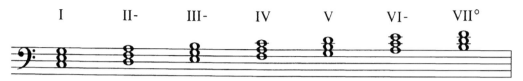

Seventh Chords

CHORD VOICINGS

Although chords are built with the root on the bottom, you can rearrange the notes so that the root is on top or in the middle. Each arrangement gives you a different *chord voicing.*

TRIADS

Triads generate three voicings. This is demonstrated below with the **I** triad. When the root is on the bottom, the triad is in *root position:*

---

[1] For those who already have some knowledge of different chord types, " - " is the symbol for *minor triads,* " ° " is the symbol for *diminished triads,* " Δ7 " is the symbol for *major-seven chords,* " -7 " is the symbol for *minor-seven chords,* " 7 " is the symbol for *dominant-seven chords,* " −7♭5 " is the symbol for *half-diminished chords,* and chords with no symbol are *major triads. Remember, you don't have to worry about these distinctions right now.*

Invert the triad by moving the root up an octave. The chord is now in *first inversion:*

Invert the triad again by moving the new bottom note up an octave. The chord is now in *second inversion:*

Invert the triad yet again, and the chord reverts back to root position (an octave higher):

Practice the three voicings of the **I** triad with your left hand, and learn to play them from memory, using the fingerings provided below. As you can see, root position, first inversion, and second inversion are now simply identified as "root," "first," and "second."

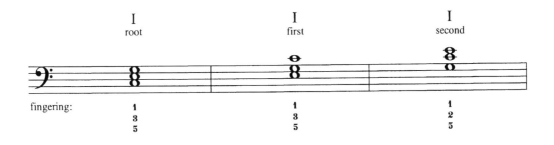

SEVENTH CHORDS

Seventh chords generate four voicings. This is demonstrated below with the **V**7 ("five-seven") chord:

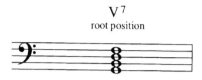

V^7
root position

V^7
first inversion

V^7
second inversion

V^7
third inversion

Practice the four voicings of the **V**7 chord with your left hand, and learn to play them from memory, using the fingerings provided below.

V^7 root	V^7 first	V^7 second	V^7 third

fingering:

1	1	1	1
2	2	2	2
3	3	3	4
5	5	5	5

MORE ON CHORD VOICINGS

So far, you've built chord inversions by starting in root position and moving the bottom note up to the top of the chord:

You can also build chord inversions by moving the top note down to the bottom of the chord:

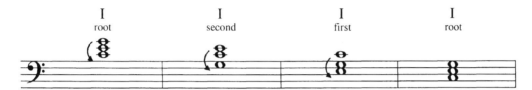

As you can see, the quickest way to build a first inversion triad is to move *up* from root position, and the quickest way to build a second inversion triad is to move *down* from root position.

Similarly, the quickest way to build a first inversion *seventh chord* is to move *up* from root position:

And the quickest way to build a third inversion seventh chord is to move *down* from root position:

(There is no advantage to moving in one direction or the other when creating second inversion seventh chords.)

When you build a chord inversion, choose the quickest route from root position to build it. Of course, once you know an inversion well, you will be able to play it without first thinking of the chord in root position. *Everything in good time.*

And now a final word about chord voicings (at least for the time being). Because root position is the first voicing you learn, it's easy to confuse the terms *root position* and *first inversion*. In order to keep these voicings straight in your mind, remember that the first inversion is the first *inverted* voicing—not the original voicing—of a chord.

THE CHORD ACCOMPANIMENT

A *chord accompaniment* is the sequence of chords used in a piece of music. This chapter's featured chord accompaniment is made up of the **I** triad in root position, and the **IV** triad in second inversion:

I   IV

root   second

Build these chords with your left hand in the octave just below middle C. (See guidelines on pages 10-13.) Check your work below.

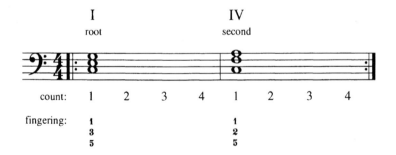

The symbols that frame the accompaniment (‖: and :‖) are repeat signs. In this context, they indicate an "open repeat," which means that the number of times you repeat the accompaniment is up to you.

Practice the chord accompaniment with your left hand and learn to play it fluently from memory. Use the fingerings provided. Choose a relaxed tempo, and count silently as you play. (Counting silently will prepare you for the upcoming improvisation—in this context, counting aloud would detract from the music.)

IMPROVISING

While counting silently, play the accompaniment introduced on the previous page. Join in with your right hand and improvise, using the following guidelines:

- Play one note at a time, drawing from the notes of the C major scale.

- Keep your rhythms simple by playing each note on a beat. (Playing between the beats will be introduced later.)

- Listen to the notes you choose in relation to the underlying chords. If you don't like the way a note sounds, simply move on to another one. If you *do* like the way a note sounds, hold on to it for a while or move to another note, as you prefer. Let your ear be your guide.

- End your improvisation on the **I** triad.

- Above all, immerse yourself in the process of improvising without becoming too concerned with the results. Everything you play will provide valuable experience.

If you like, begin your improvisation with the following excerpt, then continue with your own inventions.

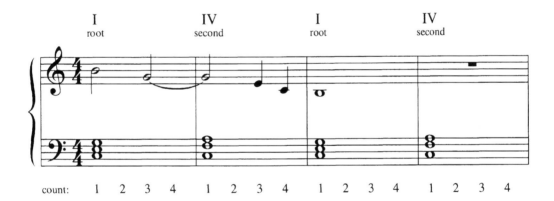

IMPROVISATION WORKSHOP

Congratulations! The improvisation you just played included the basic elements of jazz, rock, and blues piano improvising—namely, improvising over a chord accompaniment within a given meter.[1] Perhaps the results were not as compelling or fluent as you would like, but that's okay—your ability to improvise will blossom with experience.

Piano by Ear will introduce a number of improvising techniques that are key to playing jazz, rock, and blues. The techniques are introduced in a series of "Improvisation Workshops" and are illustrated with recorded and written examples. Let's get started.

IMPROVISATION WORKSHOP:

CREATING PHRASES THAT ARE SURROUNDED BY SPACE

Rather than improvise non-stop with your right hand, play distinct note sequences *(phrases)* that are separated by moments of repose *(spaces)*. The following example—which incidentally uses the same chord accompaniment you used a moment ago—illustrates phrases and spaces in action.[2] Notice that spaces are created by holding a note for an extended period of time, by not playing, or by combining these two options:

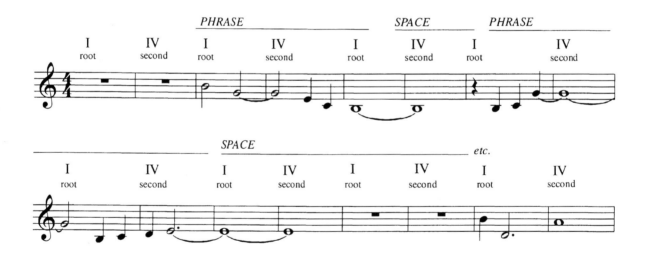

 The above example is a transcription of the opening measures of the improvisation recorded on Track 2. Read the transcription (as far as it goes) as you listen to the recording. *Notice how the spaces effectively draw you into the music by giving you a moment to reflect upon what you've just heard, and anticipate what you're about to hear. The spaces frame and compliment the phrases they surround.*

After you've listened to Track 2, return to the previous page and play another improvisation. Create phrases that are surrounded by space.

---

[1] The *meter* is the underlying rhythmic structure indicated by the time signature: 3/4, 4/4, etc.

[2] Given that you've been improvising with your right hand and playing chords with your left, you might expect the chord symbols to be written *below* the treble staff, yet writing them above the staff is standard practice.

Scale Studies

Scale Mixing

Scale Mixing is an exercise designed to help you quickly locate the notes of a scale out of sequence and identify the notes by number. This ability facilitates both building chords and improvising.

Recall that the notes of a major scale are numbered 1 through 7, and that the C major scale is numbered as follows:

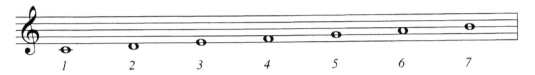

With this numbering system in mind:

- Name a note from the C major scale by number and play it.

- Name another note by number and play it with the other hand, in a different octave of the piano.

- Name yet another note and play it with the original hand, in another octave of the piano.

- Continue in this way for a minute or so. Always alternate hands and jump from one octave to another. This increases the challenge and effectiveness of the exercise.

- Play at a speed that enables you to play in a relaxed and fluent manner. Only increase your speed as your ability allows.

 Track 3 provides an example of *Scale Mixing*. The first few notes of the example are transcribed below. Read along as you listen:

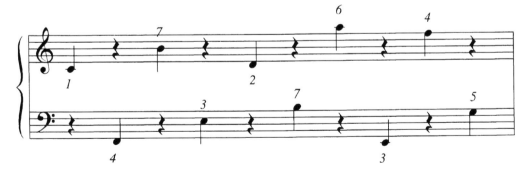

Now give *Scale Mixing* a whirl, following the above guidelines carefully. Remember that Track 3 is just an example. The notes you play—and the octaves you put them in—is up to you.

THE C MAJOR SCALE

In addition to practicing the *Scale Mixing* exercise, familiarize yourself with the C major scale by playing the notes *in order,* using the fingerings shown below.

The groups of notes labeled "three" are played with the thumb (1), second (2), and third (3) fingers, and the groups of notes labeled "four" are played with the thumb (1), second (2), third (3), and fourth (4) fingers. As you can see, playing the scale essentially involves alternating between these two finger groups. Exceptions to this rule occur either at the top of the scale (where the right hand plays the top note with the fifth finger), or the bottom of the scale (where the left hand plays the bottom note with the fifth finger).

Play the scale one hand at a time. (Playing the hands together is a lot more challenging and unnecessary for our purposes.) Choose an easy tempo so that you can play the notes evenly and smoothly. Think in terms of the finger groups described above, and learn to play the scale from memory.

right hand

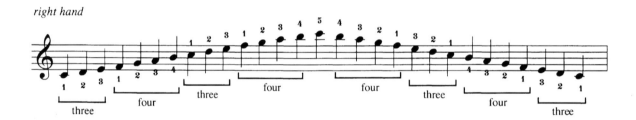

left hand

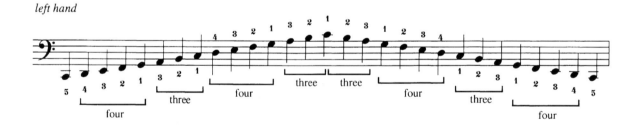

Create your own fingering when you improvise

Though important for scale practice and developing piano technique, scale fingerings only apply to improvising (and written compositions) in specific circumstances—for example, when a number of the notes of the scale are used in their original scale sequence. In general, you'll want to create your own fingerings when you improvise.

CHORD STUDIES

 This chapter introduces two chord studies devoted to developing your facility with triads and seventh chords. The first study is called *Consecutive Chords*. It's written below and demonstrated on Track 4. Listen to the recording and read along. (You don't need to play the study just yet.)

Consecutive Chords

TRIADS • Play each chord with your thumb, third, & fifth fingers (both hands).

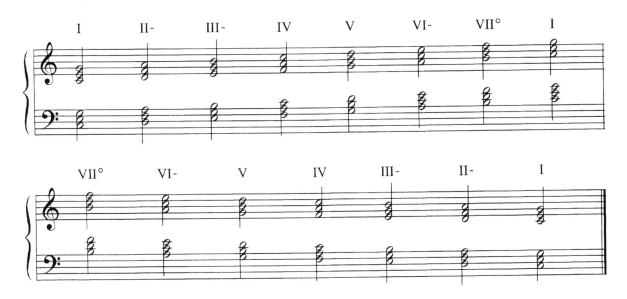

SEVENTH CHORDS • Play each chord with your thumb, second, third, & fifth fingers (both hands).

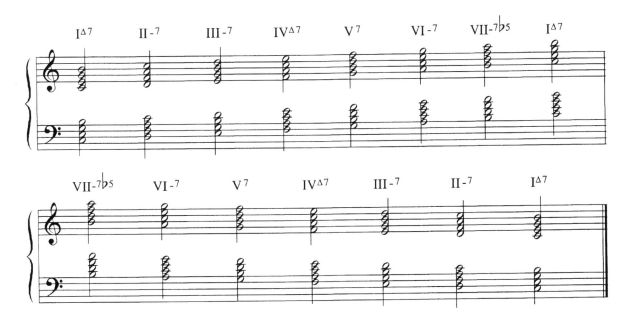

The second chord study is called *Song Pattern Chords.* It features a chord sequence that composers often draw from to harmonize their songs—sections of this chord sequence have been used in literally thousands of tunes. The study appears below and is demonstrated on Track 5. Listen to the recording and read along. (Here again, you don't need to play the study just yet.)

Song Pattern Chords

TRIADS • Play each chord with your thumb, third, & fifth fingers (both hands).

SEVENTH CHORDS • Play each chord with your thumb, second, third, & fifth fingers (both hands).

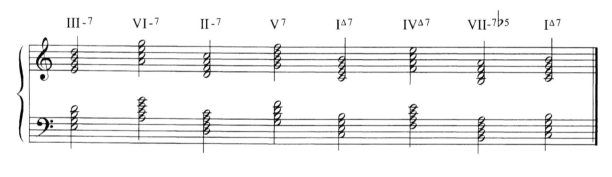

PRACTICING GUIDELINES

After listening to Tracks 4 and 5, practice the *Consecutive Chords* study and the *Song Pattern Chords* study. Follow these guidelines carefully:

- Say the name of each chord just before you play it (as demonstrated on Tracks 4 and 5). Listen closely as you play—associate the name of each chord with its sound.

- Practice your hands separately, then together.

- Choose a tempo that allows you to play without mistakes or hesitations. If a particular tempo is too challenging, slow down. It's more important to play fluently than it is to play quickly. Only increase the tempo as your ability allows.

- Learn to play the studies from memory.

LISTENING

Improvising involves a sensibility—an intuitive knowledge—that's largely developed by listening to other musicians play. Though you'll benefit the most when you set aside all distractions and immerse yourself in the music, even the most casual listening will be invaluable.

Listen frequently to the improvisation on Track 2. Remember that it uses the same accompaniment and guidelines you're using for your improvisations in this chapter.

Also listen frequently to the improvisation on Track 6. It's another improvisation created from the notes of the C major scale. This improvisation is *based* on the accompaniment and guidelines you're using, but isn't *limited* to them. You don't need to understand just how this improvisation was created, or play anything that sounds remotely like it—just listen, and know that it's directly related to the improvisation on Track 2, and to the improvisations you're creating. *Listen to Track 6 at this time.*

Finally, listen frequently to your favorite artists—both on recordings, and if possible, in concert. Become intimately familiar with the music that inspires you. Also, challenge your ears with music that's unfamiliar. Ask those whose opinion you respect for their recommendations regarding worthwhile recordings and upcoming performances.

> The improvisations on Tracks 2 and 6 are offered to inform and inspire, *not* set a standard of musicianship that you're expected to meet. Leave expectations behind! Aim to be both *alert* and completely *relaxed* when you improvise. Immerse yourself in the sounds you are creating, keeping in mind that everything you play—whether it appeals to you or not—provides valuable experience.

THE PRACTICING PAGE

Practicing frequently will help you maintain a sense of continuity from one practice session to the next. You'll find that even a ten-minute practice session can be productive—particularly when you focus on one or two activities. When time allows, practice all of the chapter's activities.[1] They're listed below:

SCALE STUDIES

Scale Mixing   p. 19
The C Major Scale   p. 20

CHORD STUDIES

Consecutive Chords   pp. 21 - 22
Song Pattern Chords   p. 22

RHYTHM STUDY

Improvising Rhythm (p. 9). This exercise lets you devote your full attention to developing important rhythm skills. You don't have any chords to contend with, and you don't even have to concern yourself with which notes you're playing.

LISTENING

 Listen to the improvisations on Tracks 2 and 6 for ideas and inspiration, and to gain an intuitive feel for the music. Remember that Track 2 was created out of the same set of guidelines you're using for your improvisations, and Track 6 is based on, but not limited to, these guidelines.

IMPROVISING

Play this chapter's accompaniment and count silently (p. 16). Join in with your right hand and improvise, drawing from the notes of the C major scale (p. 17). Create phrases that are surrounded by space (p. 18).

Play from Memory!

For best results, devote a part of each practice session to memorizing the guidelines to the activities listed above. You'll want to eventually turn to this page and practice the activities from memory. Learning the guidelines in this way will promote a solid grasp of the material, and playing from memory will strengthen your ear.

Move on to Chapter Two when you've explored the featured improvisation to your own satisfaction, and when you're able to play the scale, chord, and rhythm studies with confidence. (Remember that it's okay to play these studies slowly.) Completing the chapter may take a day or many days. Spend as much time as you need!

---

[1] Chapter Two will introduce learning the featured chord accompaniment by ear. Chapter Four will introduce learning one or more melodic phrases from a recorded improvisation by ear. It will also introduce the art of composing melodic phrases.

Chapter Two

F MAJOR

Max [Roach] plays musical lines with dynamics and space. What he doesn't play is just as important as what he does play.

—Kenny Washington
drummer

THE F MAJOR SCALE

The music in Chapter Two will be in the key of F major and created entirely from the notes of the F major scale. Imagine a keyboard that is limited to the notes of the F major scale as you play:

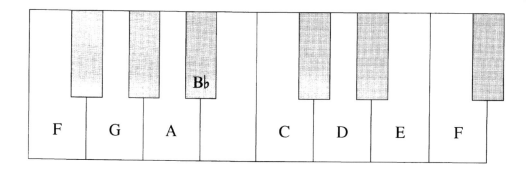

Given that a piece of music can be performed in any key, why not play everything in the easy key of C? Here are four reasons:

• Though essentially the same, each key possesses its own subtle personality. If you were to limit yourself to one key, you would sacrifice the variety that each key offers.

• A key is chosen, in part, to place a piece in an ideal range: not too high and not too low. Range is particularly critical when the voice and certain other instruments are involved, but it's also an important consideration in solo piano playing.

• Because pieces are, in fact, written in various keys, you would have to transpose them into the key of C before you could play them in C, which would be no small task.

• Even if you went to the trouble of transposing every piece into the key of C, you would end up playing in numerous keys anyway. Many pieces, although primarily in one key, visit other keys temporarily.

To avoid becoming overly attached to playing in some keys and adverse to playing in others, you'll want to gain experience in a number of keys early in your studies. Book One features eight of the twelve major keys.

THE ANATOMY OF THE MAJOR SCALE

A *half step* is the distance between any two adjacent notes on the piano; G up to G♯ is a half step; so is F down to E. Combining two adjacent half steps gives you one *whole step*. For example, combining the half step C up to D♭ and the half step D♭ up to D gives you the whole step C up to D.

All major scales conform to the same sequence of half steps (h) and whole steps (W). The sequence is illustrated here with the C major scale:

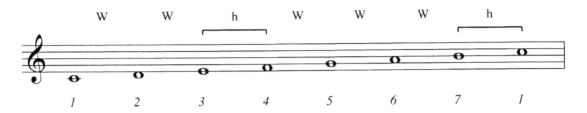

To remember this sequence, remember that *3* and *4*, and *7* and *1* are a half step apart, and the other notes are a whole step apart. The C major scale conforms to this sequence without any sharps or flats. All other major scales include at least one sharp or one flat. The F major scale includes *B♭*:

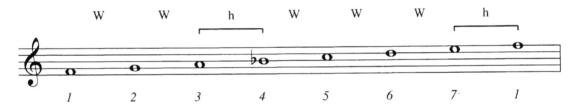

KEY SIGNATURES

The sharps or flats at the beginning of a staff constitute the *key signature*. The key signature of a major key is determined by the sharps or flats in the key's corresponding major scale. Since there's a B♭ in the F major scale, there's also a B♭ in the key signature of the key of F major.

The sharps and flats in a key signature apply to all of the corresponding notes in the music. This means that when there's a B♭ in the key signature, all of the *B's* in the music are played as *B flats*.[1] The F major key signature is used below and throughout the remainder of Chapter Two:

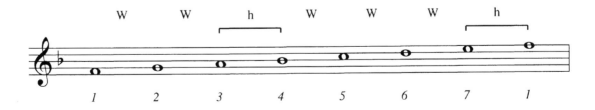

---

[1] *Accidentals* (i.e., sharp, natural, and flat signs placed in front of individual notes) are used to override the key signature. Accidentals will be used in Books Two and Three.

SCALE STUDIES

SCALE MIXING

Scale Mixing was introduced on page 19 using the C major scale. Now try it using the F major scale:

- Name a note from the F major scale by number and play it. (In the F major scale, F is *1*, G is *2*, A is *3*, B♭ is *4*, and so on.)

- Name another note by number and play it with the other hand, in a different octave of the piano.

- Name yet another note and play it with the original hand, in another octave of the piano.

- Continue in this way for a minute or so. Remember to alternate hands and to jump from one octave to another. This increases the challenge and effectiveness of the exercise.

- Play at a speed that enables you to play in a relaxed and fluent manner. Only increase your speed as your ability allows.

THE F MAJOR SCALE

Learn to play the F major scale from memory. Play one hand at a time, using the fingerings shown below. Pick an easy tempo so that you can play the scale evenly and smoothly.

Though the F major scale uses different fingerings than the C major scale, the same underlying principle is observed. Namely, that the *three-finger* group and the *four-finger* group alternate, and that any exception to this rule occurs at the top or bottom of the scale.

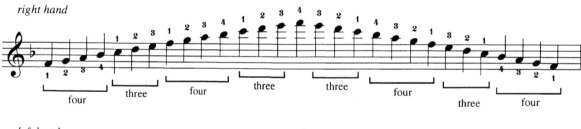

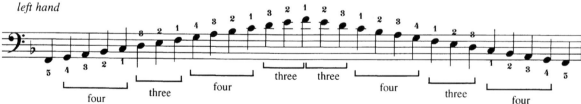

Playing scales with the recommended fingerings will develop your piano technique and, in certain circumstances, facilitate improvising. In general, however, you'll want to make up your own fingerings when you improvise.

BUILDING CHORDS

Build triads and seventh chords on the notes of the F major scale. Remember that chords are built by stacking alternate notes of the scale. Check your work below.

Triads

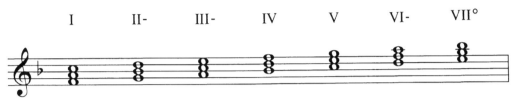

Seventh Chords

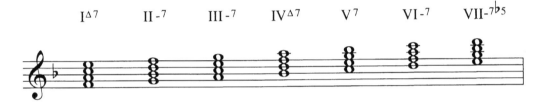

CHORD STUDIES

Use the chord studies introduced in Chapter One to practice the triads and seventh chords in F major. The studies appear on the following two pages.

Reminders:

- Say the name of each chord before you play it—associate the name with the sound.
- Practice your hands separately, then together.
- Choose a tempo that enables you to play in a relaxed and fluent manner.
- Learn to play the studies from memory.

Consecutive Chords

TRIADS • Play each chord with your thumb, third, & fifth fingers (both hands).

SEVENTH CHORDS • Play each chord with your thumb, second, third, & fifth fingers (both hands).

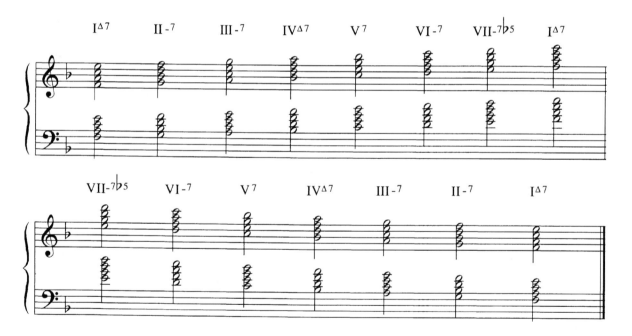

Song Pattern Chords

TRIADS • Play each chord with your thumb, third, & fifth fingers (both hands).

SEVENTH CHORDS • Play each chord with your thumb, second, third, & fifth fingers (both hands).

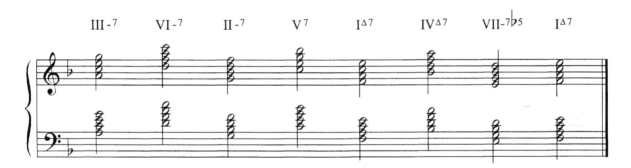

IMPROVISING RHYTHM

Chapter One introduced *Improvising Rhythm* in 4/4 time. Now try it in 3/4 time:

- Count slowly and evenly: "1 — 2 — 3 — 1 — 2 — 3" *etc.* Remember that you can count aloud or to yourself. Do whatever helps you to maintain the right number of beats in each measure.

- Play one note at a time with your right hand, drawing from the notes of the F major scale. (Your left hand doesn't play in this exercise.)

- Play each note on a beat. (Playing between the beats will be introduced later.)

- Focus on *when* you play a note—*which* note you play is of secondary importance in this exercise.

- Hold some notes into the next measure so that you're not always playing on beat 1. Doing so will produce interesting rhythms. See example below. (Remember that a curved line drawn between two notes of the same pitch is a *tie*. The second note of a tie is held over from the first note rather than played.)

- Create a variety of rhythms. You might, for example, play on beats 1, 2, and 3 in the first measure, on beat 2 in the second measure, on beats 1 and 3 in the third measure, and so on. *See how many different rhythms you can come up with as you play!*

Play for a minute or two. If you like, begin with the following example—then continue with your own inventions.

count: 1   2   3   1   2   3   1   2   3   1   2   3

> When you begin improvising within a particular meter (time signature), it's very easy to inadvertently add a beat to a measure or drop a beat from a measure. That's why counting is so important. As you gain experience with the meter, and gradually internalize it, maintaining the right number of beats per measure will require less and less conscious effort, and eventually become second nature. *Everything in good time!*

LEARNING CHORD ACCOMPANIMENTS BY EAR

Learning chord accompaniments by ear provides valuable ear training. It develops a relationship with chords based on their sound rather than simply how they look on paper. This relationship is central to playing jazz, rock, and blues.

Learning by ear often includes writing down what you hear so that you can keep track of the results—this process is referred to as *transcribing*. *Piano by Ear* will facilitate the transcribing process with step-by-step guidelines and a special recording. Always listen to the recording through headphones—they make learning by ear much easier!

This chapter's accompaniment is recorded on Track 7. As you'll hear in a moment, it includes two chords —both are triads. The low notes played in front of the chords are the roots of the chords.

Step 1   **Identify the Root**

 Slip on your headphones and play Track 7, resting a finger on the CD player's pause button. Listen to the root of the first chord (the low note at the beginning of the track), then press *pause* before the first chord is played.

With the sound of the root resonating in your ear, find it on the piano. Remember that it belongs to the F major scale. Also, know that it's located in the second octave below middle C.

Don't worry if you can't identify the root right away—just keep listening. Read on when you think that you've identified the root.

If you said that the root is F, you're right. In this key, F is the root of the I triad, so "I" is written on the line above the first measure:

 Now determine the root of the second triad. Play Track 7 and rest your finger on the pause button. Listen to the root that is played before the second triad. Press *pause* before the second triad is played.

With the sound of this root resonating in your ear, find it on the piano. Again, keep in mind that it belongs to the F major scale, and that it's located in the second octave below middle C. Try to identify the root before you read on.

The root of the second chord is B♭. B♭ is the root of the **IV** chord, so "IV" is written above the second measure:

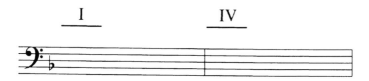

Step 2   **Identify the Top Note**

You can figure out the voicing of a chord by determining which note is on top. Begin with the first chord of the accompaniment—the **I** triad. Since this chord is composed of the notes F, A, and C, the top note is necessarily one of these three notes.

 Play Track 7 and listen to the first chord—press *pause* before the root of the second chord is played. The note of the chord you are hearing most prominently is the top note. With the sound of this note resonating in your ear, find it on the piano. Remember that the note is either F, A, or C. Also know that it's located in the general vicinity of middle C. Try to find the note before you read on.

If you said that the top note is A, you're right. A is placed in the first measure:

 Now determine the top note of the **IV** triad. Since this chord is composed of the notes B♭, D, and F, the top note is necessarily one of these three notes. Play Track 7 and listen to the second chord. The note you are hearing most prominently is the top note. With the sound of this note resonating in your ear, find it on the piano. Remember that the note is either B♭, D, or F. Also know that it's located in the general vicinity of middle C. Identify the note before you read on.

The top note of the **IV** chord is B♭, so B♭ is placed in the second measure:

Step 3   **Build the Chord from the Top Down**

Now that you know A is the top note of the **I** triad, you can build the chord from the top down. Just add the remaining two notes of the chord (F and C) directly below the A. Similarly, add the remaining two notes of the **IV** triad (F and D) below the B♭:

Step 4   **Determine the Chord Voicing**

Play the three voicings of the **I** triad, and note that the chord accompaniment that you're learning features the **I** triad in second inversion:

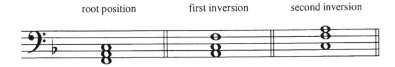

Now play the three voicings of the **IV** triad, and note that the accompaniment features the **IV** triad in first inversion:

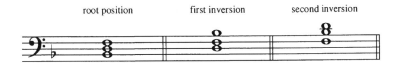

To indicate the voicings of the chords, "second" is written under the **I** triad, and "first" is written under the **IV** triad:

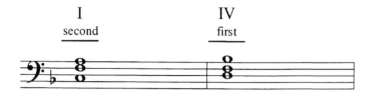

Chapter Two features this accompaniment in 3/4 time. Choose a relaxed tempo, count silently, and learn to play the accompaniment fluently from memory:

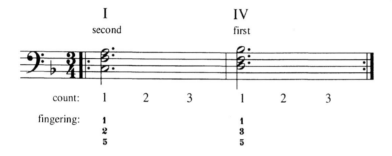

THE SUSTAIN PEDAL

As a finishing touch, use the sustain pedal (the pedal on the right) to create a smooth transition from one chord to the next. Unless you're already very experienced with pedaling, use the basic pattern of pressing the pedal down on beat 3 and letting it up on beat 1. Doing so will connect one chord to the next without blurring together the notes you'll be playing with your right hand. This pedaling pattern is illustrated below:

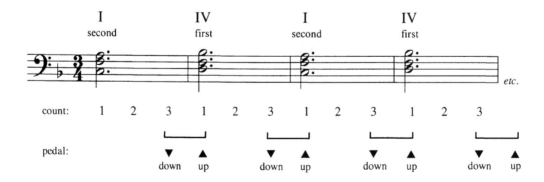

Practice the accompaniment and the pedal for a minute of two. This may be challenging at first, so be patient.

Throughout Book One, chord accompaniments will be introduced in 4/4 time, then revisited in the next chapter in 3/4 time—the chord voicings used in the two versions may differ. True to form, Chapter One introduced a 4/4 version of an accompaniment featuring the **I** and **IV** triads. Chapter Two has now introduced a 3/4 version of the same accompaniment; the voicings used in the two versions are indeed different. Looking ahead: Chapters Three and Four will share the same accompaniment, as will Chapters Five and Six, and Chapters Seven and Eight.

IMPROVISATION WORKSHOP:

VARYING THE LENGTH OF YOUR PHRASES AND SPACES

Chapter One encouraged you to play phrases that are surrounded by space. Chapter Two will encourage you to take this idea a step further by deliberately creating phrases and spaces of different lengths. Doing so will create variety and contribute to a feeling of rhythmic freedom.

Phrases that are between one and ten notes long work well. Longer phrases are also fine but are more difficult to shape and control.

Experiment with spaces that range in length from a momentary pause to a reprieve that spans three, four, or more measures. *Long spaces are very effective—they fill the listener with anticipation.*

 Listen to the improvisation on Track 8, and pay special attention to the lengths of the phrases and spaces. The first few measures of the improvisation are transcribed below. Remember: spaces are created by holding a note for an extended period of time, by not playing, or by combining these two options.

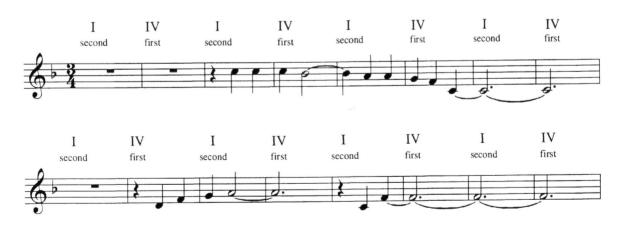

Refer to the "Improvising" section on the next page for this chapter's improvising guidelines.

THE PRACTICING PAGE

For best results, devote a part of each practice session to memorizing the guidelines to the activities listed below. You'll want to eventually turn to this page and practice the activities from memory. Learning the guidelines in this way will promote a solid grasp of the material, and playing from memory will strengthen your ear.

SCALE STUDIES

Scale Mixing   p. 28
The F Major Scale   p. 28

CHORD STUDIES

Consecutive Chords   pp. 29 & 30
Song Pattern Chords   pp. 29 & 31

RHYTHM STUDY

Improvising Rhythm (p. 32). This exercise lets you devote your full attention to developing essential rhythm skills; there are no chords to contend with, and you don't even have to concern yourself with which notes you're playing.

 ## LISTENING

Listen to the improvisation on Track 8 for ideas and inspiration, and to gain an intuitive feel for the music. This improvisation uses the same accompaniment and guidelines you're using for your improvisations.

Also listen to the improvisation on Track 9—it's based on the accompaniment and guidelines you're using, but isn't limited to them. You don't need to understand how this improvisation was created, or play anything that sounds remotely like it—just listen, and know that it's directly related to the improvisation on Track 8, and to the improvisations you're creating in this chapter.

IMPROVISING

Play this chapter's accompaniment and count silently (p. 36). Join in with your right hand and improvise, drawing from the notes of the F major scale. Keep your rhythms simple by playing each note on a count. Create phrases and spaces of different lengths (p. 37). End your improvisation on the I triad.

Immerse yourself in the process of improvising without becoming overly concerned with the results. Everything you play will provide valuable experience.

Pedal Prowess

To create a smooth transition from one chord to the next, engage the sustain pedal on beat 3 and release it on beat 1 (p. 36). If this proves to be too distracting, improvise without the pedal. Develop your *pedal prowess* by practicing the pedal and accompaniment without the right hand.

Move on to Chapter Three when you've explored the featured improvisation to your own satisfaction, and when you're able to play the scale, chord, and rhythm studies with confidence.

Chapter Three

G MAJOR

Mistakes [are a] raw material of learning. If we don't
make mistakes, we are unlikely to make anything at all.

—Stephen Nachmanovitch
from "Free Play"

THE G MAJOR SCALE

The music in Chapter Three will be in the key of G major and created entirely from the notes of the G major scale. Imagine a keyboard that is limited to the notes of the G major scale as you play:

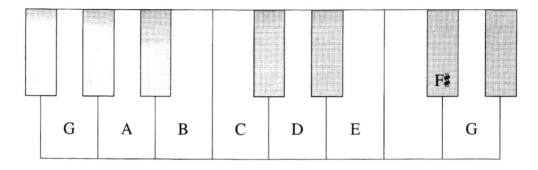

SCALE STUDIES

SCALE MIXING

Practice *Scale Mixing* in the key of G major. (In this key, G is *1*, A is *2, and so on.*) The guidelines to the exercise are on page 19.

THE G MAJOR SCALE

Learn to play the G major scale from memory. Play one hand at a time, using the fingerings shown below. (These fingerings are the same as those used for the C major scale.) Pick an easy tempo so that you can play the scale evenly and smoothly.

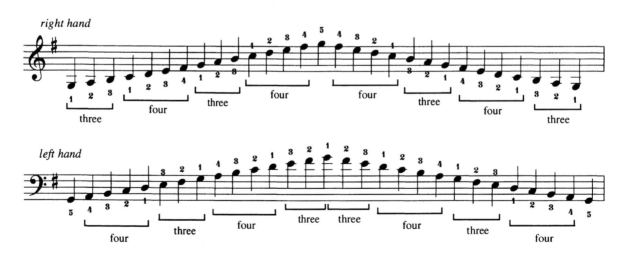

BUILDING CHORDS

Build triads and seventh chords on the notes of the G major scale. Check your work below.

Triads

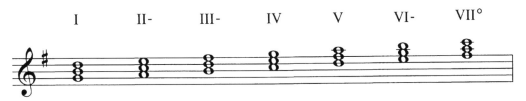

Seventh Chords

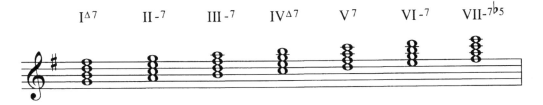

CHORD STUDIES

The *Consecutive Chords* and *Song Pattern Chords* studies on the next page are the same as those featured in the first two chapters. They look different because they're not written out note-for-note. Learn the studies in the key of G major.

Reminders:

- Say the name of each chord before you play it—associate the name with the sound.

- Play the triads with your thumb, third and fifth fingers (both hands), and the seventh chords with your thumb, second, third and fifth fingers (both hands).

- Practice your hands separately, then together. When you play the chords together, play them in adjacent octaves in the middle range of the piano.

- Choose a tempo that enables you to play in a relaxed and fluent manner.

- Learn to play the studies from memory.

Consecutive Chords

Play all chords in root position. Say the name of each chord before you play it.

Triads

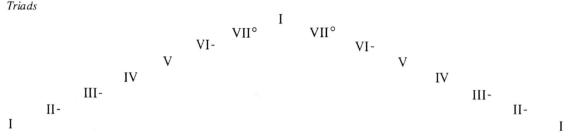

```
                                    I
                         VII°            VII°
                   VI-                         VI-
              V                                     V
         IV                                             IV
      III-                                                 III-
   II-                                                         II-
I                                                                   I
```

Seventh Chords

```
                                        IᐤΔ7
                              VII-7♭5         VII-7♭5
                      VI-7                          VI-7
                V7                                       V7
           IVΔ7                                              IVΔ7
       III-7                                                     III-7
   II-7                                                              II-7
IΔ7                                                                      IΔ7
```

Song Pattern Chords

Play all chords in root position. Say the name of each chord before you play it.

Triads

```
        VI-              V                IV
III- ↗        ↘      ↗        ↘      ↗        ↘          I
              II-              I                VII° ↗
```

Seventh Chords

```
        VI-7              V7               IVΔ7
III-7 ↗        ↘      ↗         ↘      ↗         ↘          IΔ7
               II-7              IΔ7               VII-7♭5 ↗
```

IMPROVING RHYTHM

 This *Improving Rhythm* exercise introduces eighth notes. Begin by listening to an example of the exercise on Track 10 (the "ands" on the recording represent the eighth note pulse between the beats). The first few bars of Track 10 are transcribed below so that you can follow along as you listen ("and" is written as "+"):

count: 1 + 2 + 3 + 4 +   1 + 2 + 3 + 4 +   1 + 2 + 3 + 4 + 1 + 2 + 3 + 4 +

When you're ready to continue:

- Count evenly as demonstrated on Track 10: "1 — and — 2 — and — 3 — and — 4 — and —"

- As you count, play one note at a time with your right hand, using the notes of the G major scale. (Your left hand doesn't play in this exercise.)

- Focus on *when* you play a note—*which* note you play is of secondary importance in this exercise.

- Hold some notes into the next measure so that you are not always playing on beat 1. Doing so will create interesting rhythms. (See the example above.)

New! • Play eighth notes and notes of longer value (i.e., quarter notes, whole notes, etc.) in various rhythmic combinations. *See how many different rhythms you can come up with as you play!*

- Play for a minute or two.

THE ACCOMPANIMENT

Use Track 11 and the following guidelines to learn this chapter's accompaniment by ear. As always when you transcribe, listen to the recording though headphones.

Step 1   **Identify the Root**

 Track 11 features the root of each chord just before the chord itself. Play the recording and rest your finger on the CD player's pause button. Listen to the root of the first chord. Press *pause* before the chord itself is played.

With the sound of the root resonating in your ear, find it on the piano. Remember that it belongs to the G major scale. Also, know that it's located in the second octave below middle C.

Don't worry if you can't identify the root right away—keep listening. Read on when you think you know what the root is.

_____

If you said that the root is G, you're right. G is the root of the **I** chord, so "I" is written above the first measure:

I

 Use the above approach to determine the Roman numerals in the remaining three measures. Write your answers above the lines provided. Check your work on the next page.

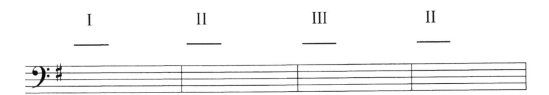

All of the chords in this accompaniment are seventh chords. Turn to the *Building Chords* section on page 41 and notice that, "△7" is added to **I**, and "-7" is added to both **II** and **III**. (Don't worry about what these symbols mean just yet; they'll be explained in Book Two.)

Step 2   **Identify the Top Note**

You can figure out the voicing of a chord by determining which note is on top. Begin with the first chord of the accompaniment—the **I**△7. Since this chord is composed of the notes G, B, D, and F♯, the top note is necessarily one of these four notes.

Play Track 11 and listen to the first chord. Press *pause* before the root of the second chord is played. The note you are hearing most prominently is the top note. With the sound of this note resonating in your ear, find it on the piano—it's located in the general vicinity of middle C. Find the note before you read on.

_____

If you said that the top note is B, you're right. B is placed in the first measure:

Use the above approach to determine the top notes of the other chords in the accompaniment. Fill in your answers above. Check your work on the next page.

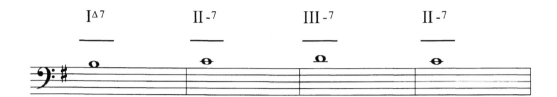

Step 3 Build the Chord from the Top Down

Now that you know B is the top note of the I∆7 chord, you can build the chord from the top down. Just add the remaining notes of the chord (G, F♯, and D) below the B:

Build the other chords from the top down. Fill in the notes above. Check your work below.

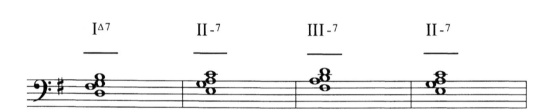

Step 4 Determine the Chord Voicing

Play the four voicings of the I∆7:

As you can see, the accompaniment you are learning features the I∆7 chord in second inversion. To indicate this, "second" is written under the I∆7:

Use the above approach to determine the voicings of the other chords in the accompaniment. Fill in your answers above. Check your work on the next page.

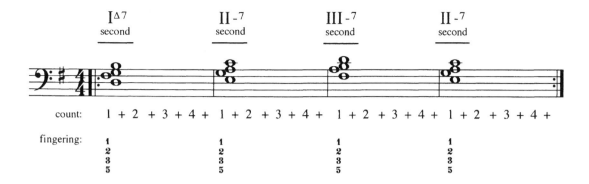

Learn to play the accompaniment fluently from memory. Choose a relaxed tempo and count silently; remember the "and" between each beat. Play the chords softly so that they'll recede into the background when you improvise. Use the sustain pedal to create a smooth transition from one chord to the next—engage the pedal on beat 4 and release it on beat 1.

IMPROVISATION WORKSHOP:

BEGINNING PHRASES ON DIFFERENT BEATS

As your left hand faithfully plays chords on the first beat of each measure, create phrases with your right hand that begin on various beats of the measure. Doing so—together with including phrases and spaces of different lengths—will create rhythmic variety and contribute to a sense of rhythmic freedom.

The first few measures of Track 12 are transcribed below. As indicated by the arrows, the first phrase begins on beat 3, the second phrase begins on beat 2, the third phrase begins on beat 4, and so on. Listen to the improvisation—notice on which beat the phrases begin.

Refer to the "Improvising" section on page 49 for this chapter's improvising guidelines.

THE DIFFERENT BEAT EXERCISE

The following exercise will develop your skill at beginning phrases on different beats of the measure. As you can see below, the same three-note phrase begins on beat 1 of the first measure, on beat 2 of the third measure, on beat 3 of the fifth measure, and on beat 4 of the seventh measure.

 Listen to the exercise on Track 13. Notice that even though the phrase is repeated note-for-note, placing it on different beats subtly changes its character. Also notice that placing it on different beats creates a feeling of rhythmic freedom over the rhythmically predictable accompaniment.

Learn to play the exercise from memory.

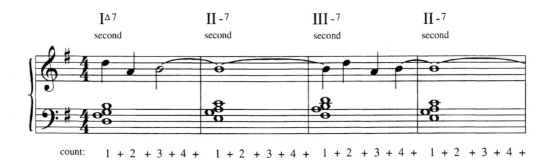

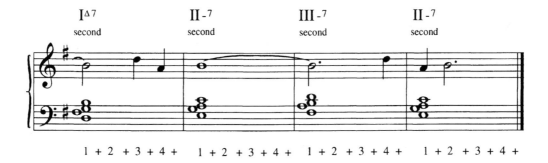

THE PRACTICING PAGE

Playing *by heart* will strengthen your ear. For best results, learn to play the following activities from memory:

SCALE STUDIES

Scale Mixing   p. 40
The G Major Scale   p. 40

CHORD STUDIES

Consecutive Chords   pp. 41 & 42
Song Pattern Chords   pp. 41 & 42

RHYTHM STUDIES

Improvising Rhythm   p. 43
The Different Beat Exercise   p. 48

LISTENING

Listen to the improvisations on Tracks 12 and 14 for ideas and inspiration, and to gain an intuitive feel for the music. Track 12 was created out of the same set of guidelines you're using for your improvisations. Track 14 is based on, but not limited to, these guidelines.[1]

IMPROVISING

Play this chapter's accompaniment with your left hand and count silently (p. 47). Join in with your right hand and improvise, drawing from the notes of the G major scale. End your improvisation on the I∆7 chord. Let your ear be your guide when you improvise. Also, make use of these techniques:

New! • Begin phrases on different beats of the measure

New! • Include eighth notes

• Vary the length of your phrases and spaces

Immerse yourself in the process of improvising without becoming overly concerned with the results. Everything you play will provide valuable experience.

Pedal Prowess (Revisited)

To create a smooth transition from one chord to the next, engage the pedal on beat 4 and release it on beat 1. If this proves to be too distracting, improvise without the pedal. Develop your pedaling prowess by practicing the pedal and accompaniment without the right hand.

---

[1] Track 14 includes a few notes that are not in the G major scale. *Going outside the scale* will be addressed in Book Two.

Chapter Four

B♭ MAJOR

My brother, Jimmie, and I would learn music note-for-note from records: Everyone from B.B. King, Buddy Guy, and Bo Diddley to the Stones and the Beatles.

—Stevie Ray Vaughan
guitarist

THE B♭ MAJOR SCALE

The music in Chapter Four will be in the key of B♭ major and created entirely from the notes of the B♭ major scale. Imagine a keyboard that is limited to the notes of the B♭ major scale as you play:

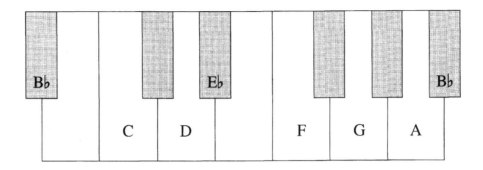

SCALE STUDIES

SCALE MIXING
Guidelines: page 19

Practice *Scale Mixing* in the key of B♭ major.

THE B♭ MAJOR SCALE

Learn to play the B♭ major scale from memory. Play one hand at a time, using the fingerings shown below. Pick an easy tempo so that you can play the scale evenly and smoothly.

right hand

left hand

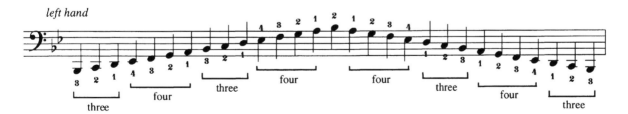

BUILDING CHORDS

Build triads and seventh chords on the notes of the B♭ major scale. Check your work below.

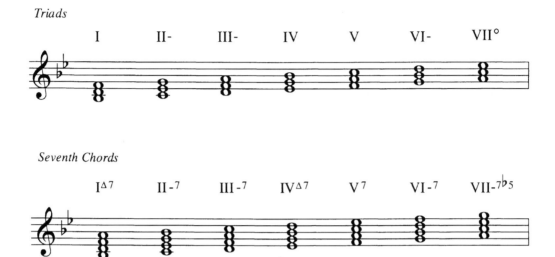

Triads

I   II-   III-   IV   V   VI-   VII°

Seventh Chords

I△7   II-7   III-7   IV△7   V7   VI-7   VII-7♭5

CHORD STUDIES

Learn to play *Consecutive Chords* (triads and seventh chords) and *Song Pattern Chords* (triads and seventh chords) from memory in the key of B♭ major. Remember to say the name of each chord before you play it. The guidelines to these chord studies are on pages 41-42.

IMPROVISING RHYTHM

This *Improvising Rhythm* exercise introduces eighth notes in 3/4 time:

- Count slowly and evenly: "1 — and — 2 — and — 3 — and —" *etc.*

- As you count, play one note at a time with your right hand using the notes of the B♭ major scale. (Your left hand doesn't play in this exercise).

- Focus on *when* you play a note—*which* note you play is of secondary importance in this exercise.

- Hold some notes into the next measure so that you are not always playing on beat 1.

- Play eighth notes and notes of longer value in various rhythmic combinations. *See how many different rhythms you can come up with as you play!*

- Play for a minute or two.

THE ACCOMPANIMENT

This accompaniment was introduced in Chapter Three:

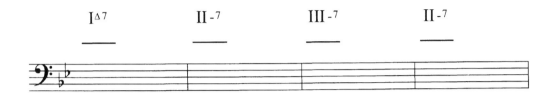

In addition to the new key, the chord voicings may differ from those used in Chapter Three. Figure out the voicings from Track 15. Here's a reminder of how you can do this:

- **Identify the Top Notes**

   Begin with the I△7. Since the top note is necessarily one of the notes in the chord, start by determining which notes are in the chord; you can do this by building the I△7 in root position. Now, listen to Track 15 and push *pause* after you hear the first chord. The note you're hearing most prominently is the top note. With the sound of this note resonating in your ear, find it on the piano—it's located in the general vicinity of middle C. Once you've determined the identity of the note, write it in the first measure on the staff above. Use the same approach to identify the top notes of the other three chords.

- **Build the Chords from the Top Down**

   Return to the I△7. Now that you know that the top note is D, you can build the chord from the top down—just add the remaining notes of the chord (B♭, A, and F) below the D. Use the same approach to build the other three chords from the top down.

- **Identify the Voicings**

   Play the I△7 in all of its voicings. As you can see, second inversion is used in the above accompaniment. Write "second" just below "I△7." Repeat this process for the other three chords.

Check your work on the next page.

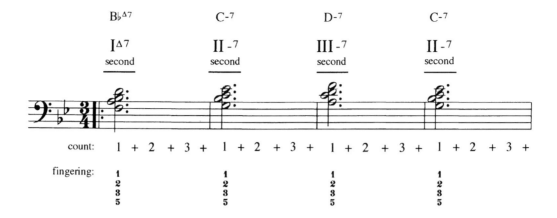

Learn to play the accompaniment fluently from memory. Choose a relaxed tempo and count silently. Play the chords softly so that they'll recede into the background when you improvise. Use the sustain pedal to create a smooth transition from one chord to the next—engage the pedal on beat 3 and release it on beat 1.

Chords can be identified by *letter name* as well as by Roman numeral. Letter names are simple: if the root of a chord is B♭, the letter name of that chord is "B♭"; if the root is C, the letter name is "C," and so on. The chords in the above accompaniment are identified by letter name and by Roman numeral. Notice that the attached symbols (" 7," etc.) are the same in each instance.

Letter names are useful because they're easy to grasp. Roman numerals are useful because they will help you to:

- understand how chords function within a piece of music

- recognize and recall common chord sequences, regardless of the key

- identify chords by ear

The value of Roman numerals will become increasingly evident as the course unfolds. In order to benefit fully from *Piano by Ear*, continue to think of chords in terms of their Roman numeral names.

INCORPORATING PHRASES FROM RECORDED IMPROVISATIONS

This workshop will show you how to learn phrases directly from the recorded improvisations and will encourage you to incorporate these phrases into your own improvisations.

- Learning the phrases will strengthen your ear, provide insight into the featured improvisations, and help prepare you for learning directly from the improvisations of your favorite artists.

- Incorporating the phrases into your improvisations will challenge and sharpen your musical memory, add variety to your improvising, and perhaps spark your imagination in ways that lead your improvising in new directions.

Piano by Ear's approach to learning and transcribing (writing down) phrases is presented in five steps. The guidelines enclosed in a box apply to the transcribing process in general. The guidelines that are *not* in a box apply to the first phrase of Track 16, which is the phrase you'll be transcribing in a moment. Listen to the recording through headphones when you transcribe.

Step 1

Choose a phrase that you like from the recorded improvisation. If your CD player has a *minute/second* display, jot down the time displayed at the start of your phrase. This will enable you to find the phrase easily.

To learn the phrase, press *pause* after the first note. With this note resonating in your ear, find it on your keyboard; then jot it down on the upper staff. (As you can see below, an upper staff and a lower staff are provided for the transcription.) Don't concern yourself with the rhythm right now. For clarity, make your notes small, centering them carefully on the appropriate line or in the appropriate space.

Repeat Step 1 for each note in the phrase. *You may discover that you can figure out more than one note at a time—if so, you won't need to stop the recording after each note.*

 Using the above guidelines, figure out the notes of Track 16's first phrase and jot them down on the upper staff. The first three notes of the phrase have been transcribed for you:

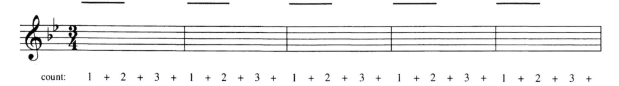

count: 1 + 2 + 3 +   1 + 2 + 3 +   1 + 2 + 3 +   1 + 2 + 3 +   1 + 2 + 3 +

Check your work on the next page.

The notes in Track 16's first phrase are:

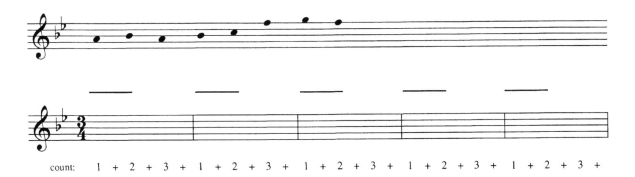

count: 1 + 2 + 3 + 1 + 2 + 3 + 1 + 2 + 3 + 1 + 2 + 3 + 1 + 2 + 3 +

Step 2

> Listen to the improvisation and tap the beats with your left hand:
>
> • tap beat 1 with your thumb
> • tap beat 2 with your 2nd (index) finger
> • tap beat 3 with your 3rd (middle) finger
> • and when an improvisation is in 4/4 time, tap beat 4 with your 4th (ring) finger
>
> It's *very helpful* to watch your fingers as you tap so that you can, in effect, see the beats as well as hear them. It's also helpful to tap on your thigh so that you can feel the beats in your body.
>
> Two measures of percussion are played before the improvisation begins. Start tapping in the second measure as shown below. Keep in mind that once the improvisation begins, your thumb will tap each time a chord is played.

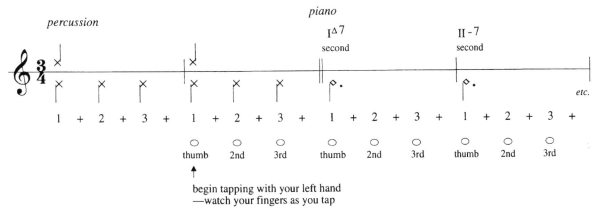

 Play Track 16, *watch your fingers,* and tap the beats as described above.

Step 3

Begin listening to the recording a few measures before the phrase you are learning. Tap the beats and watch your fingers as you did in Step 2. When the first note of the phrase is played, observe the position of your fingers:

- A note that sounds as you tap your thumb falls on beat 1.
- A note that sounds after you tap your thumb, but before you tap your index finger, falls on the "and" of beat 1.
- A note that sounds as you tap your index finger falls on beat 2, and so on.

Once you've figured out the rhythmic placement of the first note, write it above the appropriate beat in the first measure of the lower staff.

Repeat Step 3 for each note of the phrase.

 Play Track 16, tap the beats, watch your fingers, and notice that the first note of the first phrase is played as you tap your index finger. This tells you that the note falls on beat 2. Consequently, the note is placed above the "2" in the first measure of the lower staff (see staffs below).

Now return to Track 16, tap the beats, watch your fingers, and notice that the second note of the phrase is played after you tap your index finger, but before you tap your middle finger, revealing that the note falls on the "and" of beat 2. Therefore, the note is placed above the "+" between beats 2 and 3.

Repeat Step 3 for each note of the phrase. Write down the notes above the appropriate counts as you go. This work is challenging—please be patient!

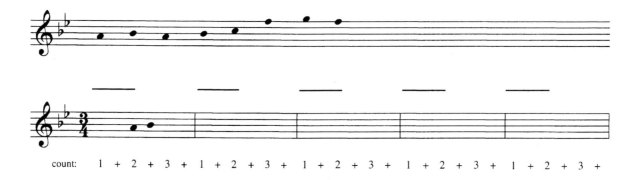

count: 1 + 2 + 3 +   1 + 2 + 3 +   1 + 2 + 3 +   1 + 2 + 3 +   1 + 2 + 3 +

Check your work on the next page.

count: 1 + 2 + 3 + 1 + 2 + 3 + 1 + 2 + 3 + 1 + 2 + 3 + 1 + 2 + 3 +

Step 4

> Listen to the recording and figure out which chord is being played when the phrase
> begins. Write this chord on the line above the first measure. Once you've figured out the
> first chord, you can fill in the other chords since you already know the order of the
> chords in the accompaniment.

  Listen to Track 16 and figure out which chord is being played when the first phrase begins.
Write the chord (either **I**Δ7, **II**-7, or **III**-7) on the line above the first measure. Now fill in the
other chords by relying on your knowledge of the accompaniment. (The accompaniment is on
page 54.)

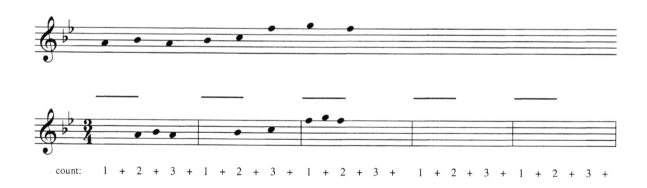

count: 1 + 2 + 3 + 1 + 2 + 3 + 1 + 2 + 3 + 1 + 2 + 3 + 1 + 2 + 3 +

Check your work on the next page.

The phrase begins in the **III-7** measure of the accompaniment. Consequently, **III-7** is written above the first measure; **II-7** (the next, and last, chord of the accompaniment) is written above the second measure; and **IΔ7** (the beginning of a new cycle of the accompaniment) is written above the third measure:

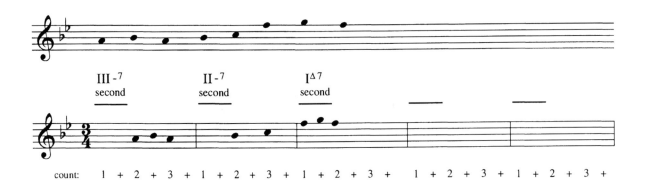

Step 5

> Learn to play the phrase (together with the chords) fluently from memory. Incorporate it into your own improvisations.

Learn to play Track 16's first phrase from memory, and incorporate it into your own improvisations.

INCORPORATING PHRASES THAT YOU'VE COMPOSED

In addition to the phrase you've just transcribed from Track 16, compose one of your own phrases and transcribe it below.

- Composing is a great way to enhance your improvising skills—it gives you an opportunity to experiment with note combinations and rhythms without having to contend with the moment-to-moment demands of improvising.

- Incorporating your composed phrases into your improvisations will challenge and sharpen your musical memory, anchor your improvisations with music that is *tried and true*, and serve as a springboard for the phrases you create while improvising.

You can use essentially the same transcribing method you used to transcribe from the CD:

- Write down the notes of the phrase on the upper staff.
- Position the notes above the appropriate beats on the lower staff.
- Determine which chords accompany the phrase and write them on the lines provided.

WORKSHOP PROJECT

Compose your own phrase on the staffs below. If you like, begin with a rough draft and modify it to taste. (Write lightly in pencil and keep an eraser handy.) Remember to make your notes small and to center them carefully on the appropriate line or in the appropriate space. Learn to play the phrase (with the chords) fluently from memory and include it in your improvisations.

count: 1 + 2 + 3 + 1 + 2 + 3 + 1 + 2 + 3 + 1 + 2 + 3 + 1 + 2 + 3 +

> Don't become too concerned with composing a *great* phrase. The point here is to gain experience with transcribing musical ideas. *Creating masterpieces is strictly optional.*

THE PRACTICING PAGE

Playing *by heart* will strengthen your ear. For best results, learn to play the following activities from memory:

SCALE STUDIES

CHORD STUDIES

RHYTHM STUDY

LISTENING

Listen to the improvisations on Tracks 16 and 17 for ideas and inspiration, and to gain an intuitive feel for the music. Track 16 was created out of the same set of guidelines you're using for your improvisations. Track 17 is based on, but not limited to, these guidelines.

IMPROVISING

Play this chapter's accompaniment with your left hand and count silently (p. 54). Join in with your right hand and improvise, drawing from the notes of the B♭ major scale. End your improvisation on the I△7 chord. *Let your ear be your guide when you improvise.* Also, make use of the techniques listed below. (Rather than consider all of these techniques at once, you can shift your focus from one to another, or if you prefer, create a number of short improvisations and explore a different technique in each one.)

New! • Include the phrase from Track 16 that you've memorized (p. 60), and the phrase of your own that you've memorized (p. 61)

• Begin phrases on different beats of the measure

• Vary the length of your phrases and spaces

• Include eighth notes

Musicianship and Creativity

The usefulness of learning phrases from recordings and composing phrases, then weaving these phrases into your improvisations, cannot be overstated. The practice is invaluable for both enhancing musicianship and nurturing creativity.

Chapter Five

D MAJOR

You need repetition as a basic part of musical form, but what you want is both repetition and development.... Artists are always juggling such things, either instinctively or analytically.

—Chuck Israels
bassist

THE D MAJOR SCALE

The music in Chapter Five will be in the key of D major and created entirely from the notes of the D major scale. Imagine a keyboard that is limited to the notes of the D major scale as you play:

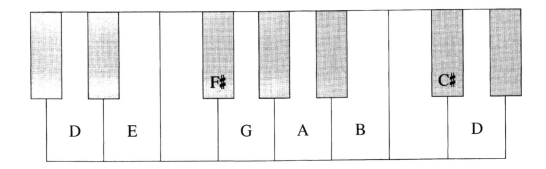

SCALE STUDIES

SCALE MIXING
Guidelines: page 19

Practice *Scale Mixing* in the key of D major.

THE D MAJOR SCALE

Learn to play the D major scale from memory. Play one hand at a time, using the fingerings shown below. (The fingerings are identical to those used for the C major scale.) Pick an easy tempo so that you can play the scale evenly and smoothly.

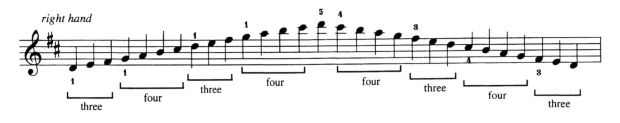

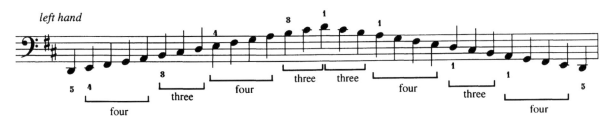

BUILDING CHORDS

Build triads and seventh chords on the notes of the D major scale. Check your work below.

Triads

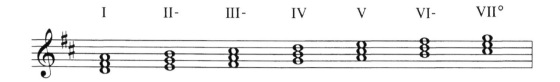

Seventh Chords

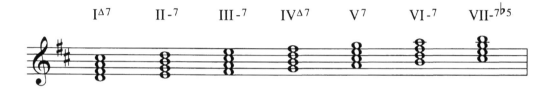

CHORD STUDIES

Guidelines: pages 41-42

Learn to play *Consecutive Chords* (triads and seventh chords) and *Song Pattern Chords* (triads and seventh chords) from memory in the key of D major.

EIGHTH-NOTE SYNCOPATION

Playing on a *beat* means playing on a count, and playing on an *off-beat* means playing on an "and":

· In previous chapters, notes played on off-beats were sandwiched between notes played on the two surrounding beats. For example, notes played on the "and" of beat 1 were surrounded by notes played on beats 1 and 2:

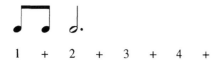

If you remove one or both notes played on the surrounding beats, you will draw attention to— and effectively emphasize—the off-beat. The *x's* in the following illustration indicate where a surrounding note has been removed (or where it has been tied to the previous note so that it's held rather than played):

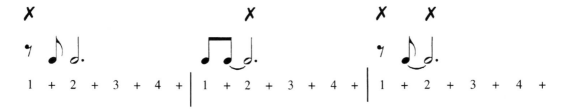

Drawing attention to an off-beat (by not playing on one or both surrounding beats) is a rhythmic effect called *eighth-note syncopation.* Eighth-note syncopation is native to jazz, rock, and blues —it contributes to the spontaneity and rhythmic drive of the music.

IMPROVISING RHYTHM

Eighth-note syncopation is featured in this chapter's *Improvising Rhythm* exercise:

- Count slowly and evenly in 4/4 time: "1 — and — 2 — and — 3 — and — 4 — and —" *etc.*

- As you count, play one note at a time with your right hand using the notes of the D major scale. (Your left hand does not play in this exercise.)

- Focus on *when* you play a note—*which* note you play is of secondary importance in this exercise.

- Hold some notes into the next measure so that you are not always playing on beat 1.

New! • Memorize the following two syncopated rhythms and include them in your *Improvising Rhythm* practice. (Don't limit yourself to a single note when you play the rhythms—use various notes of the D major scale.)

New! • Make up your own rhythms that feature eighth-note syncopation. *See how many different rhythms you can come up with!*

- Play for a minute or two.

THE ACCOMPANIMENT

This chapter's accompaniment has two sections. Section A is made up of triads, and Section B is made up of seventh chords.

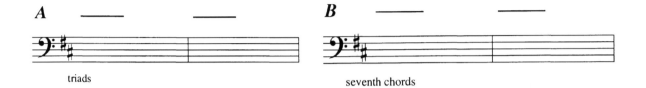

triads   seventh chords

Learn the accompaniment from Track 18 and transcribe it above. (You will hear a momentary pause between Section A and Section B.) The transcribing guidelines are summarized below. Look back to pages 44-47 for additional guidance.

Step 1   **Identify the Root**

Listen to the root of the first chord, and press *pause* before the chord itself is played. Find the note on the piano, keeping in mind that the note belongs to the chapter's featured major scale and is located in the second octave below middle C. Once you've identified the root, write the corresponding Roman numeral above the first measure—leave room beneath the Roman numeral so you'll have room to write in the voicing (root, first, etc.). Repeat Step 1 for the other chords in the accompaniment.

Step 2   **Identify the Top Note**

Return to the first chord. Since the top note of a voicing is necessarily one of the notes in the chord, start by determining which notes are in the first chord; you can do this by building the chord in root position. Then, listen to the recording and push *pause* after you hear the chord. The note you hear most prominently is the top note. Find it on the piano and write it in the first measure—it's located in the general vicinity of middle C. Repeat Step 2 to identify the top notes of the other chords in the accompaniment.

Step 3   **Build the Chord from the Top Down**

Now that you know the top note of the first chord, you can build the chord from the top down—just add the remaining notes of the chord below the top note. Repeat Step 3 to build the other chords from the top down.

Step 4   **Identify the Voicings**

Determine the voicing of the first chord (root, first, etc.) and write it underneath the Roman numeral of the first measure. Repeat Step 4 for the other chords in the accompaniment.

Check your work on the next page.

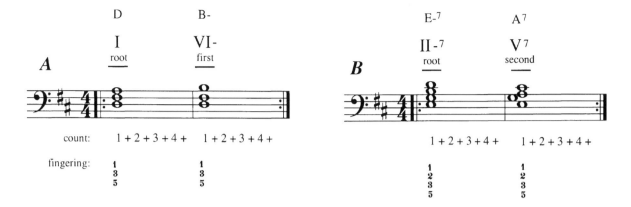

Learn to play the accompaniment fluently from memory. Count silently, play the chords softly, and use the sustain pedal to create a smooth transition from one chord to the next. Engage the pedal on beat 4 and release it on beat 1.

When you improvise over the accompaniment, stay within each section for as long as you like. You may want to repeat Section A three of four times before moving on to Section B. Then again, you may want to repeat Section A a dozen times before you move on. Do whatever sounds good in the moment.

Go back and forth between sections as many times as you like: A – B – A – B, and so on. End your improvisations on the **I** triad after either section.

IMPROVISATION WORKSHOP:
REPEATING PHRASES AND PARTS OF PHRASES

Previous Improvisation Workshops have introduced ways of creating variety within an improvisation: Chapter Two suggested creating phrases and spaces of varied length, and Chapter Three encouraged you to begin phrases on different beats of the measure. Creating variety is basic to the art of improvisation. Equally important is creating a sense of continuity, which is largely accomplished through the use of repetition. This workshop will explore repeating phrases and parts of phrases.

 The first two phrases of the improvisation recorded on Track 19 begin with the same few notes. Listen to the two phrases on the recording, and notice how this use of repetition creates a sense of continuity from one phrase to the next. The phrases are transcribed below:

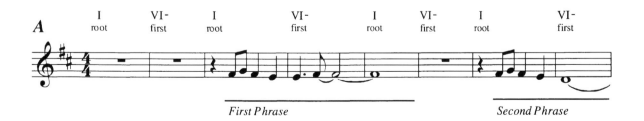

REPEATING PARTS OF PHRASES

Play this chapter's improvisation accompaniment with your left hand (see top of previous page). Join in with your right hand and create pairs of phrases that are partially the same. The phrases can begin the same and end differently—as in the example on the previous page—or they can begin differently and end the same. Explore both possibilities.

When you create a pair of phrases that you particularly like, transcribe the phrases below. Use the transcribing approach introduced in Chapter Four (page 61); remember that the upper staff is used for jotting down notes without regard for the rhythm, and the lower staffs are used for placing the notes above the appropriate beats and off-beats. Also remember to write the chord symbols on the lines provided. This transcribing approach is illustrated at the bottom of this page with two phrases that begin differently and end the same.

When you transcribe your pair of phrases, take care to leave the desired number of counts between the two phrases. You will only need to use the third staff if your two phrases span more than the five measures provided by the second staff. Write lightly in pencil and keep an eraser handy—you may want to modify your phrases after you transcribe them. Learn to play your phrases (with the chords) fluently from memory and incorporate them into your improvisations.

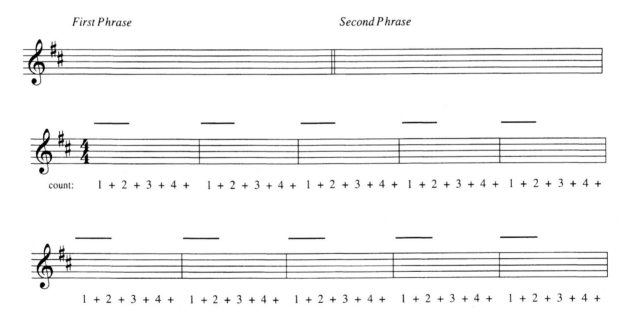

Transcription Example:

REPEATING ENTIRE PHRASES

In addition to repeating parts of phrases, experiment with repeating complete phrases. You can repeat a phrase right away, or wait until after you've played one or more other phrases. Whatever you do, make the original phrase simple so that it'll be easy to repeat.

I and *V7*

Like all of the improvisations in *Piano by Ear,* this chapter's improvisation ends on a **I** chord. The **I** chord is the chord that compositions gravitate to and typically end on. It's the *chord of resolution.*

By way of contrast, the **V7** chord has a restless and unstable sound that—more than any other chord derived form the major scale—produces tension and an expectation for resolution to a **I** chord. The **V7** and **I** chords are the quintessential chords of harmonic tension and release.

To demonstrate the characteristics of the **V7** and **I** chords, create a short improvisation using Section B of this chapter's accompaniment. Stop on the **V7** chord and notice that the improvisation sounds unresolved and incomplete. To resolve the tension of the **V7** chord, and give the improvisation a sense of completion, play the **I** triad.

TRANSCRIBING FROM TRACK 19

 Use the following staffs to transcribe a phrase or two from Track 19 that you particularly like. The transcribing guidelines are on pages 55-60. (These guidelines illustrate tapping the beats of each measure in 3/4 time; tapping the beats in 4/4 time is illustrated at the bottom of this page.)

count: 1 + 2 + 3 + 4 + 1 + 2 + 3 + 4 + 1 + 2 + 3 + 4 + 1 + 2 + 3 + 4 + 1 + 2 + 3 + 4 +

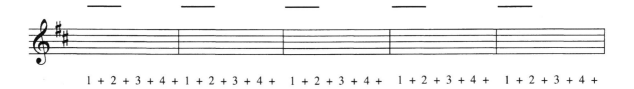

1 + 2 + 3 + 4 + 1 + 2 + 3 + 4 + 1 + 2 + 3 + 4 + 1 + 2 + 3 + 4 + 1 + 2 + 3 + 4 +

Once you've transcribed the phrase(s) from Track 19, turn to the transcription of the recording on pages 74-75 and check your work. Learn to play one phrase (with the chords) fluently from memory, and incorporate it into your own improvisations.

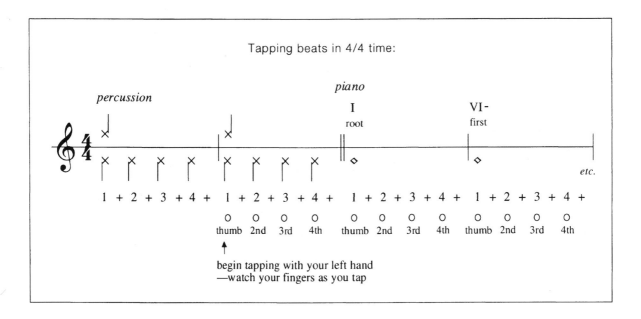

THE PRACTICING PAGE

Learn to play the following activities from memory:

SCALE STUDIES

Scale Mixing   p. 64
The D Major Scale   p. 64

CHORD STUDIES

Consecutive Chords   p. 65
Song Pattern Chords   p. 65

RHYTHM STUDY

Improvising Rhythm   p. 67

LISTENING

Listen to the improvisations on Tracks 19 and 20 for ideas and inspiration, and to gain an intuitive feel for the music. Track 19 was created out of the same set of guidelines you're using for your improvisations. Track 20 is based on, but not limited to, these guidelines.

IMPROVISING

Play this chapter's accompaniment with your left hand and count silently (p. 69). Join in with your right hand and improvise, drawing from the notes of the D major scale. End your improvisation on the I triad. *Let your ear be your guide when you improvise.* Also, make use of the techniques listed below.

New! • Repeat phrases and parts of phrases

New! • Include eighth-note syncopation, particularly the two rhythms featured in this chapter's *Improvising Rhythm* exercise (p. 67)

• Include the phrase from Track 19 that you've memorized (p. 72), and the pair of phrases of your own that you've memorized (p. 70)

• Begin phrases on different beats of the measure

• Vary the length of your phrases and spaces

Spontaneity may have to take a back seat when you use the improvising techniques listed above. That's okay—as you gain experience with the techniques and gradually internalize them, you'll develop the ability to use them in ways that serve your intuitive feeling for the music you're creating. *Remember that you can shift your focus from one technique to another when you improvise rather than consider all of the techniques at once.*

TRANSCRIPTION OF TRACK 19

Find the phrase(s) that you've transcribed and check your work.

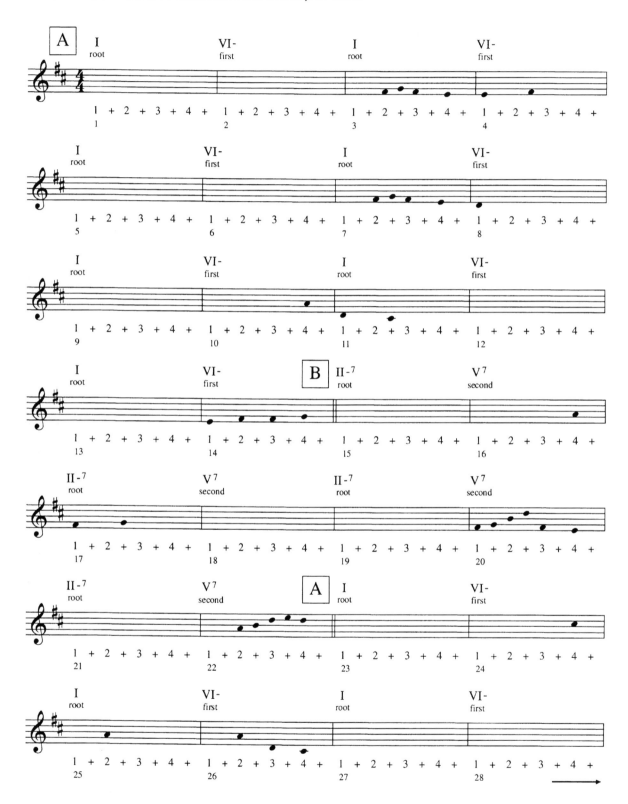

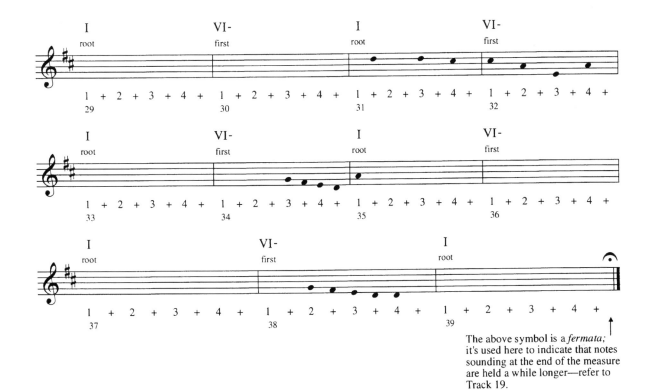

The above symbol is a *fermata;* it's used here to indicate that notes sounding at the end of the measure are held a while longer—refer to Track 19.

To benefit further from this transcription, listen to Track 19 and read along. Keep your eyes and ears peeled for examples of the featured improvising techniques (listed in the "Improvising" section on page 73). Notice, for example, that the phrase in measure 14 and the phrase in measures 16-17 end with the same two notes (F♯ and G). Listen to how this use of repetition creates continuity.

Chapter Six

E♭ MAJOR

You see spontaneity is not the same as differentness. You don't have to play something different every time for it to be spontaneous. The only prerequisite for spontaneity is having all of one's attention on the moment. It's fully experiencing the world around you.

—Chick Corea
pianist

THE E♭ MAJOR SCALE

The music in Chapter Six will be in the key of E♭ major and created entirely from the notes of the E♭ major scale. Imagine a keyboard that is limited to the notes of the E♭ major scale as you play:

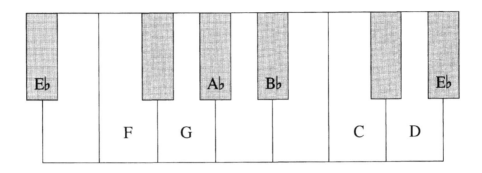

SCALE STUDIES

SCALE MIXING
Guidelines: page 19

Practice *Scale Mixing* in the key of E♭ major.

THE E♭ MAJOR SCALE

Learn to play the E♭ major scale from memory. Play one hand at a time. Choose an easy tempo so that you can play the scale evenly and smoothly.

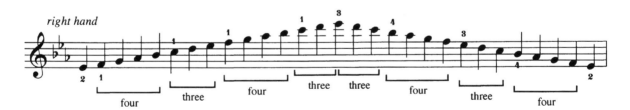

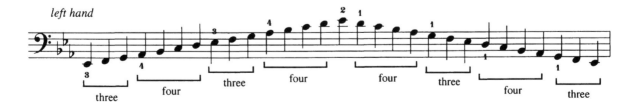

BUILDING CHORDS

Build triads and seventh chords on the notes of the E♭ major scale. Check your work below.

Triads

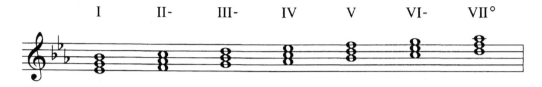

Seventh Chords

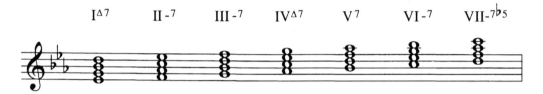

CHORD STUDIES

Guidelines: pages 41-42

Learn to play *Consecutive Chords* (triads and seventh chords) and *Song Pattern Chords* (triads and seventh chords) from memory in the key of E♭ major.

IMPROVISING RHYTHM

This *Improvising Rhythm* exercise introduces eighth-note syncopation in 3/4 time:

- Count slowly and evenly in 3/4 time: " 1 — and — 2 — and — 3 — and —"   *etc.*

- As you count, play one note at a time with your right hand using the notes of the E♭ major scale. (Your left hand does not play in this exercise.)

- Focus on *when* you play a note—*which* note you play is of secondary importance in this exercise.

- Hold some notes into the next measure so that you are not always playing on beat 1.

New! • Memorize the following two syncopated rhythms and include them in your *Improvising Rhythm* practice. (Don't limit yourself to a single note when you play the rhythms.)

- Make up your own rhythms that feature eighth-note syncopation. *See how many different rhythms you can come up with!*

- Play for a minute or two.

THE ACCOMPANIMENT

 This accompaniment was introduced in Chapter Five. Since the voicings used here may differ from those used in Chapter Five, figure out the voicings from Track 21 and indicate them below. (See Steps 2 through 4 on page 68 for guidance.) Check your work on the next page.

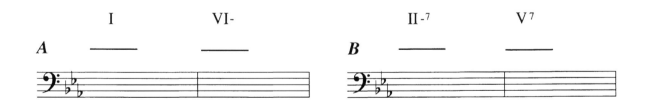

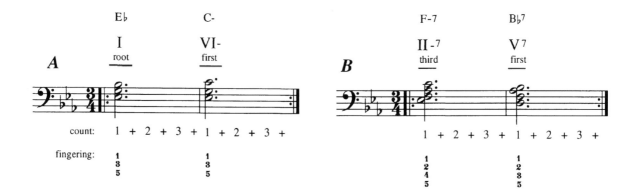

Learn to play the accompaniment fluently from memory. Count silently, play the chords softly, and use the sustain pedal to create a smooth transition from one chord to the next. Engage the pedal on beat 3 and release it on beat 1.

When you improvise over the accompaniment, stay within each section for as long as you like, and go back and forth between sections as many times as you like: A - B - A - B, and so on. End your improvisations on the I triad after either section.

REPEATING MELODIC CONTOURS AND RHYTHMIC PATTERNS

Like the Workshop in Chapter Five, this Workshop will explore the use of repetition as a means of creating continuity. Specifically, it will explore the repetition of *melodic contours* and *rhythmic patterns.*

 Listen to the first two phrases of the improvisation recorded on Track 22. Notice that the second phrase echoes the first and how this creates a sense of continuity. The phrases are transcribed below:

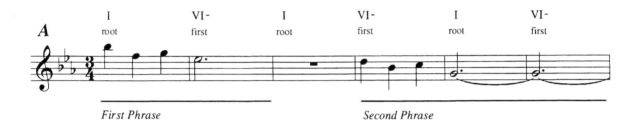

Given that these phrases are made up of different notes, why do they sound related?

• First, they sound related because they share similar melodic contours. To illustrate this, draw a line from one note to the next within each of the two phrases. You'll see that the resulting shapes, or *contours,* are about the same:

• The phrases also sound related because they share similar rhythms:

Notice that the contours and rhythms of the two phrases are not identical. That's okay; as long as they're similar, they will be heard as a repetition.

WORKSHOP PROJECT
Guidelines: page 61

Play this chapter's accompaniment with your left hand (page 80). Join in with your right hand and create pairs of phrases that share similar melodic contours and rhythms. When you create a pair that you particularly like, transcribe the phrases on the staffs below.

Remember that the upper staff is intended for jotting down phrases without regard for rhythm, and the lower staffs are intended for placing the notes of the phrases above the appropriate counts. Fill in the chord symbols on the lines provided. Write lightly in pencil and keep an eraser handy—you may want to modify your phrases after you transcribe them.

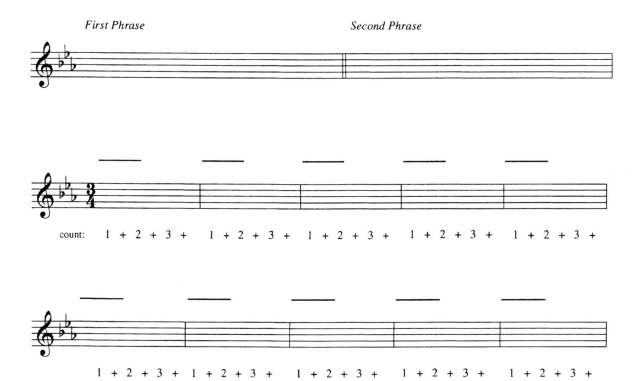

Learn to play the phrases (with the chords) fluently from memory and incorporate them into your improvisations.

REPEATING ONLY THE RHYTHM

Listen to the third, fourth and fifth phrases of Track 22 and notice that the three phrases sound related. The phrases are transcribed below:

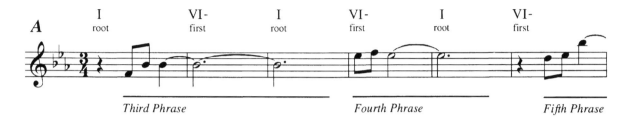

Though the contours of these phrases are dissimilar, a sense of continuity is created by the repeated rhythmic pattern:

WORKSHOP PROJECT
Guidelines: page 61

Play this chapter's accompaniment. Join in with your right hand and create pairs of phrases with similar rhythms and *dissimilar* contours. When you create a pair that you particularly like, transcribe the phrases on the staffs below.

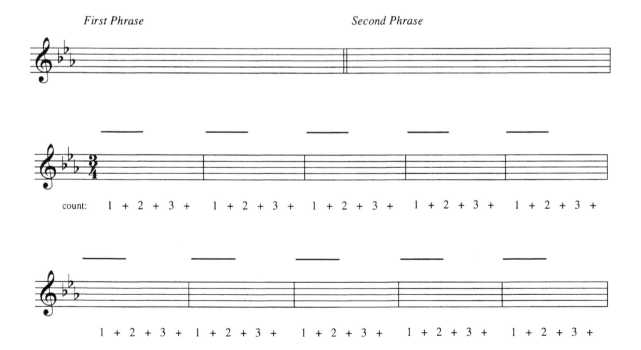

TRANSCRIBING FROM TRACK 22

Guidelines: pages 55-60

Transcribe a phrase or two from Track 22 that you particularly like. Find the phrase(s) on pages 86-87 and check your work. Learn to play one phrase (with the chords) fluently from memory and incorporate it into your own improvisations.

count: 1 + 2 + 3 +   1 + 2 + 3 +   1 + 2 + 3 +   1 + 2 + 3 +   1 + 2 + 3 +

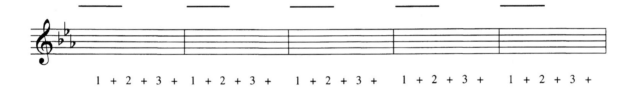

1 + 2 + 3 + 1 + 2 + 3 +   1 + 2 + 3 +   1 + 2 + 3 +   1 + 2 + 3 +

THE PRACTICING PAGE

Learn to play the following activities from memory:

SCALE STUDIES

CHORD STUDIES

RHYTHM STUDY

LISTENING

Listen to the improvisations on Tracks 22 and 23 for ideas and inspiration, and to gain an intuitive feel for the music. Track 22 was created out of the same set of guidelines you're using for your improvisations. Track 23 is based on, but not limited to, these guidelines.

IMPROVISING

Play this chapter's accompaniment with your left hand and count silently (p. 80).

Join in with your right hand and improvise, drawing from the notes of the E♭ major scale. End your improvisation on the I triad. Let your ear be your guide when you improvise. Also, make use of these techniques:

New! • Repeat melodic contours and rhythmic patterns

• Repeat phrases and parts of phrases

• Include eighth-note syncopation, particularly the two rhythms featured in this chapter's *Improvising Rhythm* exercise (p. 79)

• Include the phrase from Track 22 that you've memorized (p.84), and the pair of phrases of your own that you've memorized (p.82)

• Begin phrases on different beats of the measure

• Vary the length of your phrases and spaces

Don't Hold Back!

Along with including phrases that you've transcribed, you may find yourself playing phrases that you've played before. Don't hold back! There's a common misconception that everything in an improvisation should be brand new, but in reality, even the most accomplished and innovative artists combine familiar phrases—or parts of familiar phrases—with those they create in the moment.

---

[1] Track 23 includes a few notes that are not in the E♭ major scale.

TRANSCRIPTION OF TRACK 22

Find the phrase(s) that you've transcribed and check your work.

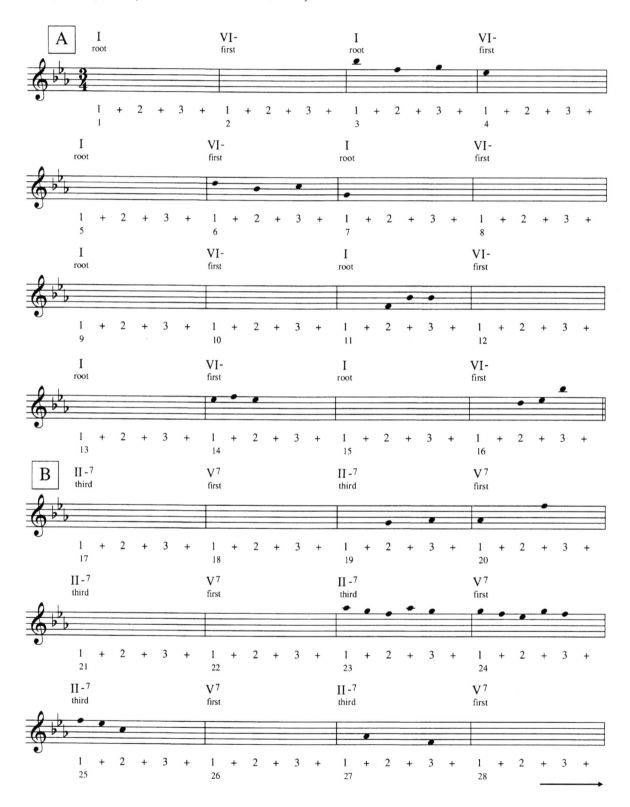

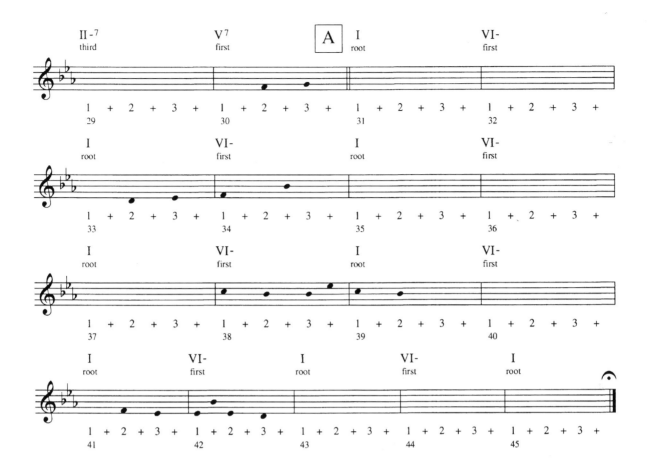

 To benefit further from this transcription, listen to Track 22 and read along. Keep your eyes and ears peeled for examples of the featured improvising techniques. Notice, for example, that the melodic contour and rhythm of the phrase in measures 38-39 resembles the contour and rhythm of the phrase in measures 41-42. Listen to how this repetition creates a sense of continuity. Also notice that the two phrases begin on different beats of their respective measures, and how this *rhythmic displacement* provides variety and a sense of rhythmic freedom over the rhythmically predictable accompaniment.

Chapter Seven

Ab MAJOR

I got into jazz...by listening to all the happening players and analyzing what they did.... To understand what a soloist did in a certain part of the music, I'd write it out.

—Herbie Hancock
pianist

THE A♭ MAJOR SCALE

The music in Chapter Seven will be in the key of A♭ major and created entirely from the notes of the A♭ major scale. Imagine a keyboard that is limited to the notes of the A♭ major scale as you play:

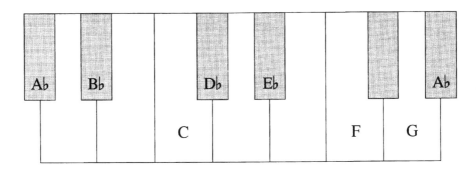

SCALE STUDIES

SCALE MIXING
Guidelines: page 19

Practice *Scale Mixing* in the key of A♭ major.

THE A♭ MAJOR SCALE

Learn to play the A♭ major scale from memory. Play one hand at a time. Choose an easy tempo so that you can play the scale evenly and smoothly.

right hand

left hand

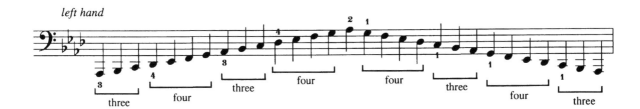

BUILDING CHORDS

Build triads and seventh chords from the notes of the A♭ major scale. Check your work below.

Triads

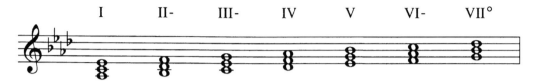

Seventh Chords

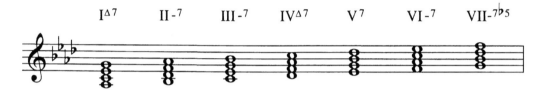

CHORD STUDIES

Guidelines: pages 41-42

Learn to play *Consecutive Chords* (triads and seventh chords) and *Song Pattern Chords* (triads and seventh chords) from memory in the key of A♭ major.

IMPROVISING RHYTHM

An important form of eighth-note syncopation involves playing on the last eighth note of a measure, then holding the note into the next measure. This form of eighth-note syncopation is explored in the following *Improvising Rhythm* exercise.

- Count slowly and evenly in 4/4 time: "1 — and — 2 — and — 3 — and — 4 — and —" *etc.*

- As you count, play one note at a time with your right hand using the notes of the A♭ major scale. (Your left hand doesn't play in this exercise.)

- Focus on *when* you play a note—*which* note you play is of secondary importance in this exercise.

New! - Memorize the following rhythm and include it in your *Improvising Rhythm* practice. Notice that the note played on the "and" of beat 4 is held into the next measure:

New! - Make up your own rhythms in which notes played on the "and" of beat 4 are held into the next measure.

- Play for a minute or two.

THE ACCOMPANIMENT

Guidelines: page 68

 Learn the accompaniment from Track 24 and transcribe it below. The chords in the first six measures are triads; the chords in the last two measures are seventh chords. Check your work on the next page.

triads ⟶

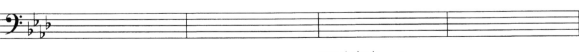

seventh chords ⟶

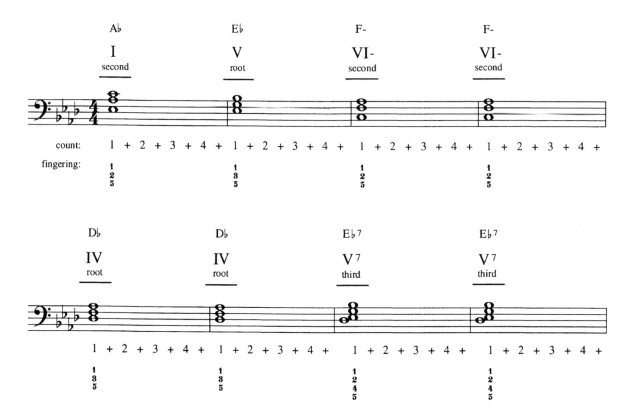

Learn to play the accompaniment fluently from memory. Count silently, play the chords softly, and use the sustain pedal to create a smooth transition from one chord to the next.

Improvisation Workshop:
Filling Out the Accompaniment

Filling out the accompaniment will refer to repeating a chord—or some part of a chord—after it has been played on the first beat of a measure.

The first few measures of the improvisation recorded on Track 25 are transcribed below, and the different ways in which the accompaniment has been *filled out* are identified. Notice that many of the measures have been left *unfilled*. Study the transcription—then listen to the recording. (The brackets below the staffs will be explained on the next page.)

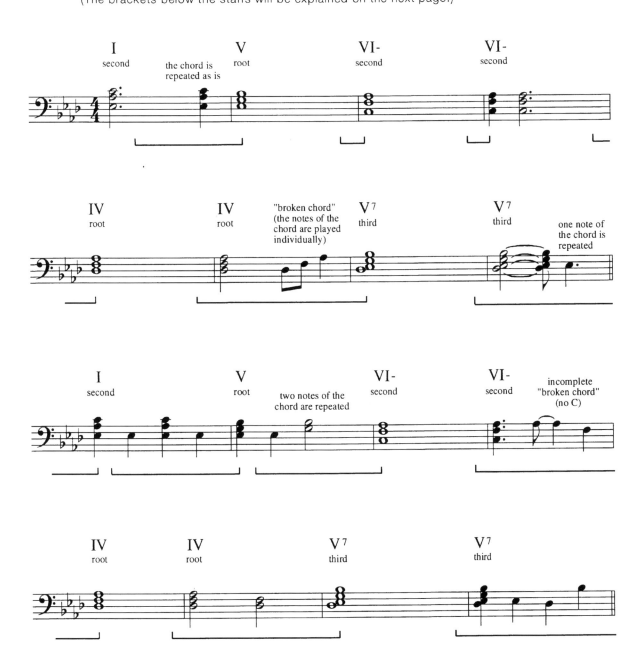

PEDALING

Students not already experienced in the art of pedaling have been encouraged to engage the sustain pedal on the last beat of a measure and release it on the first beat of the following measure. Doing so connects one chord to the next without blurring together too many of the notes being played with the right hand.

Now, you might also explore using the pedal to sustain the notes of a chord when you're filling out the accompaniment. In the example below, the pedal is used to sustain the first chord while the notes of the chord are repeated one-by-one. Since the notes belong to the same chord, pedaling them together will not compromise the clarity of the chord. (Avoid pedaling together notes of different chords.) Pedaling is indicated with a bracket below the staff—the pedal is engaged where the bracket begins and released where the bracket ends:

 Return to Track 25 and listen to the pedal in action. The brackets on the previous page show how the pedal is used in the first sixteen bars.

Be Stingy

It's better to use too little pedal than too much. Be particularly stingy with the pedal when you're improvising (right hand) and filling out the accompaniment (left hand) at the same time. When in doubt, you can always revert back to engaging the pedal on the last beat of a measure and releasing it on the first beat of the following measure.

Using the transcription on page 93 as a general guide, practice filling out this chapter's accompaniment. After you've played a chord on beat 1, you're free to repeat the chord—or any part of the chord—anywhere in the remainder of the measure. Leave some measures unfilled— they will provide a welcome contrast to the measures you *do* fill. Experiment with the sustain pedal as discussed on the previous page.

Transcribe one of your filled-out accompaniments below; the first measure has been filled out for you. As always, indicate the rhythm by placing the notes over the appropriate beats and off-beats.

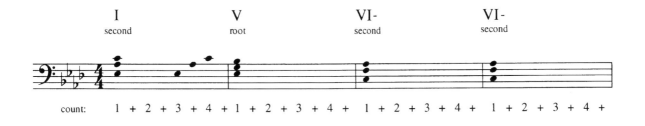

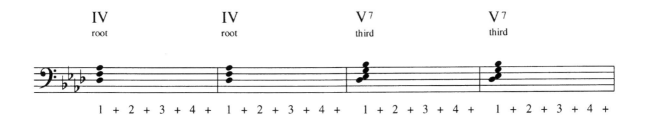

Learn to play some part of your filled-out accompaniment from memory, and incorporate it into your improvisations.

TRANSCRIBING FROM TRACK 25

Guidelines: pages 55-60

 Shift your focus back to the right hand, and transcribe a phrase or two from Track 25 that you particularly like—keep in mind that the notes in a chord that are played one-at-a-time belong to the filled-out accompaniment rather than the phrase you're transcribing. Find the phrase(s) on pages 98-99 and check your work. Learn to play one phrase fluently from memory and incorporate it into your own improvisations.

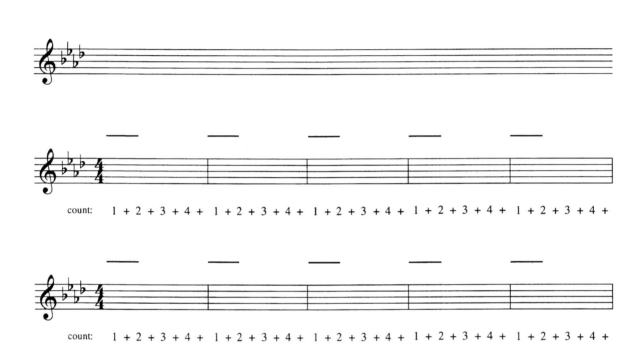

count: 1 + 2 + 3 + 4 +   1 + 2 + 3 + 4 +   1 + 2 + 3 + 4 +   1 + 2 + 3 + 4 +   1 + 2 + 3 + 4 +

count: 1 + 2 + 3 + 4 +   1 + 2 + 3 + 4 +   1 + 2 + 3 + 4 +   1 + 2 + 3 + 4 +   1 + 2 + 3 + 4 +

THE PRACTICING PAGE

Learn to play the following activities from memory:

SCALE STUDIES

Scale Mixing   p. 89
The A♭ Major Scale   p. 89

CHORD STUDIES

Consecutive Chords   p. 90
Song Pattern Chords   p. 90

RHYTHM STUDY

Improvising Rhythm   p. 91

LISTENING

Listen to the improvisations on Tracks 25 and 26 for ideas and inspiration, and to gain an intuitive feel for the music. Track 25 was created out of the same set of guidelines you're using for your improvisations. Track 26 is based on, but not limited to, these guidelines. [1]

IMPROVISING

Play this chapter's accompaniment with your left hand and count silently (p. 92). Join in with your right hand and improvise, drawing from the notes of the A♭ major scale. End your improvisation on the I triad. Let your ear be your guide when you improvise. Also, make use of these techniques:

New! • Fill out the accompaniment

- Repeat melodic contours and rhythmic patterns

- Repeat phrases and parts of phrases

- Include eighth-note syncopation, particularly the rhythm featured in this chapter's *Improvising Rhythm* exercise (p. 91)

- Include the phrase from Track 25 that you've memorized (p. 96), and the part of the filled-out accompaniment that you've composed and memorized (p. 95)

- Begin phrases on different beats of the measure

- Vary the length of your phrases and spaces

Ease Into It

Filling out the accompaniment while improvising is challenging! Ease into the challenge by only filling out the accompaniment when your right hand is leaving a space between phrases. Make some of your spaces extra long (say, from four to eight measures) so that in these instances you can devote your undivided attention to your left hand.

---

[1] Track 26 includes a few notes that are not in the A♭ major scale.

TRANSCRIPTION OF TRACK 25

Find the phrase(s) that you have transcribed and check your work. (This transcription begins with the entrance of the right hand. The first sixteen measures of the improvisation are played by the left hand only and are transcribed on page 93.)

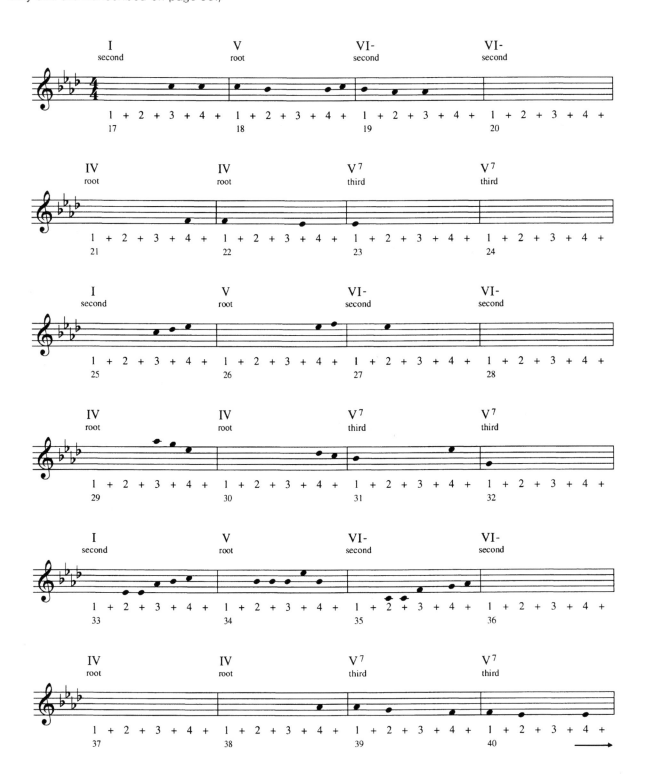

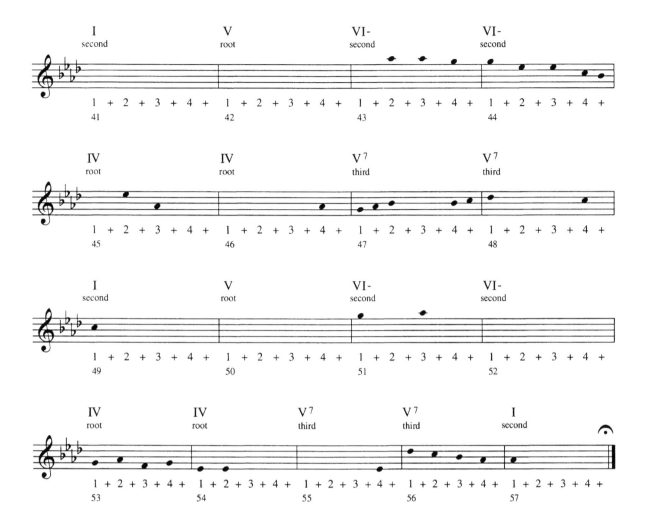

 To benefit further from this transcription, listen to Track 25 and read along. Keep your eyes and ears peeled for examples of the featured improvising techniques. Also notice the interplay between the filled-out accompaniment and the right-hand phrases, and how your attention shifts from one to the other.

Chapter Eight

D♭ MAJOR

My development was a gradual thing. I didn't wake up one day and have it. As you grow older, you realize that you've got tomorrow. When I was younger, I used to hear [Art] Blakey and [Thelonious] Monk say that: "Well, we've got tomorrow. We can try it again."

—Gary Bartz
saxophonist

THE D♭ MAJOR SCALE

The music in Chapter Eight will be in the key of D♭ major and created entirely from the notes of the D♭ major scale. Think of the scale as all five black keys plus the notes F and C:

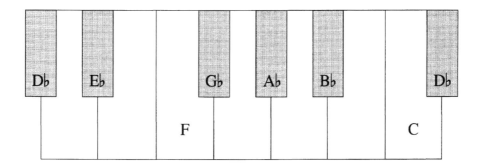

SCALE STUDIES

SCALE MIXING
Guidelines: page 19

Practice *Scale Mixing* in the key of D♭ major.

THE D♭ MAJOR SCALE

Learn to play the D♭ major scale from memory. Play one hand at a time. Choose an easy tempo so that you can play the scale evenly and smoothly.

right hand

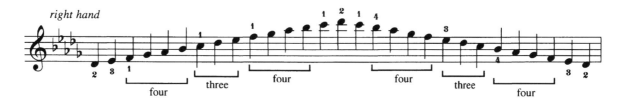

left hand

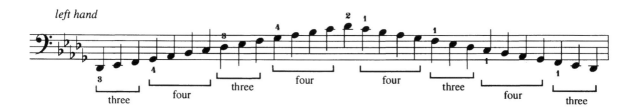

BUILDING CHORDS

Build triads and seventh chords from the notes of the D♭ major scale. Check your work below.

Triads

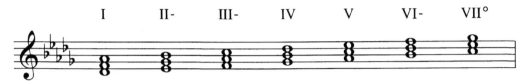

Seventh Chords

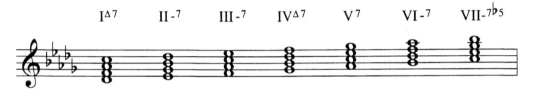

CHORD STUDIES

Guidelines: pages 41-42

Learn to play *Consecutive Chords* (triads and seventh chords) and *Song Pattern Chords* (triads and seventh chords) from memory in the key of D♭ major.

IMPROVISING RHYTHM

Like the previous chapter's *Improvising Rhythm* exercise, this one encourages you to include rhythms in which you play on the last eighth note of a measure, then hold the note into the next measure:

- Count slowly and evenly in 3/4 time: "1 — and — 2 — and — 3 — and —"   *etc.*

- As you count, play one note at a time with your right hand using the notes of the D♭ major scale. (Your left hand does not play in this exercise.)

- Focus on *when* you play a note—*which* note you play is of secondary importance in this exercise.

New! • Memorize the following rhythm and include it in your *Improvising Rhythm* practice. Notice that the note played on the "and" of beat 3 is held into the next measure:

New! • Make up your own rhythms in which notes played on the "and" of beat 3 are held into the next measure.

- Play for a minute or two.

THE ACCOMPANIMENT

Guidelines: page 68

 This accompaniment was introduced in Chapter Seven. The voicings used here may differ from those used in Chapter Seven. Figure out the voicings from Track 27, and transcribe them below. Check your work on the next page.

I	V	VI-	VI-

IV	IV	V⁷	V⁷

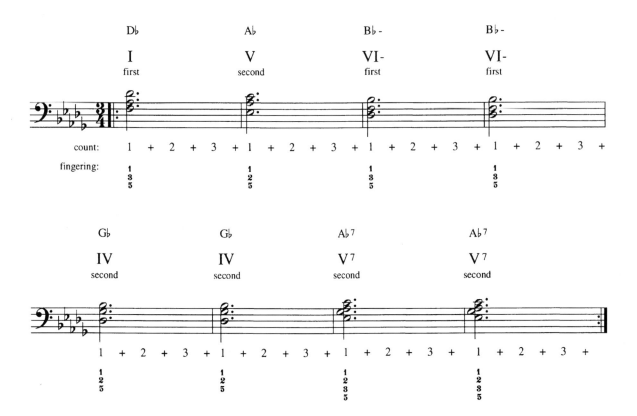

Learn to play the accompaniment fluently from memory. Count silently, play the chords softly, and use the sustain pedal to create a smooth transition from one chord to the next.

TRANSCRIBING

Guidelines: pages 55-61

 Transcribe a phrase or two from Track 28 that you particularly like—remember that the notes in a chord that are played one-at-a-time belong to the filled-out accompaniment rather than the phrase you're transcribing. Find the phrase(s) on pages 107-108 and check your work. Learn to play one phrase fluently from memory and include it in your own improvisations.

count: 1 + 2 + 3 +   1 + 2 + 3 +   1 + 2 + 3 +   1 + 2 + 3 +   1 + 2 + 3 +

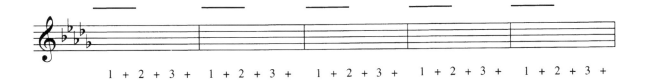

1 + 2 + 3 +   1 + 2 + 3 +   1 + 2 + 3 +   1 + 2 + 3 +   1 + 2 + 3 +

Compose a phrase or two on the staffs below. Learn to play one phrase fluently from memory and incorporate it into your improvisations.

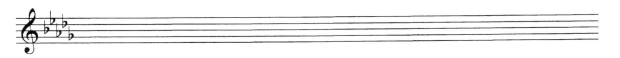

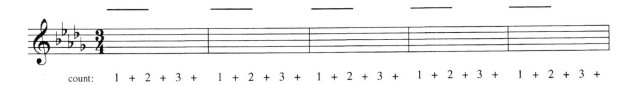

count: 1 + 2 + 3 +   1 + 2 + 3 +   1 + 2 + 3 +   1 + 2 + 3 +   1 + 2 + 3 +

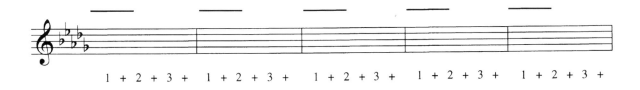

1 + 2 + 3 +   1 + 2 + 3 +   1 + 2 + 3 +   1 + 2 + 3 +   1 + 2 + 3 +

THE PRACTICING PAGE

Learn to play the following activities from memory:

SCALE STUDIES

Scale Mixing   p. 101
The D♭ Major Scale   p. 101

CHORD STUDIES

Consecutive Chords   p. 102
Song Pattern Chords   p. 102

RHYTHM STUDY

Improvising Rhythm   p. 103

LISTENING

Listen to the improvisations on Tracks 28 and 29 for ideas and inspiration, and to gain an intuitive feel for the music. Track 28 was created out of the same set of guidelines you're using for your improvisations. Track 29 is based on, but not limited to, these guidelines.

IMPROVISING

Play this chapter's accompaniment with your left hand and count silently (p. 104).

Join in with your right hand and improvise, drawing from the notes of the D♭ major scale. End your improvisation on the I triad. Let your ear be your guide when you improvise. Also, make use of these techniques:

- Fill out the accompaniment

- Repeat melodic contours and rhythmic patterns

- Repeat phrases and parts of phrases

- Include eighth-note syncopation, particularly the rhythm featured in this chapter's *Improvising Rhythm* exercise (p.103)

- Include the phrase from Track 28 that you've memorized (p.105), and the phrase of your own that you've memorized (p.105)

- Begin phrases on different beats of the measure

- Vary the length of your phrases and spaces

Leaving Long Spaces

Remember that you can leave the accompaniment *unfilled* when your right hand is playing a phrase. Leave long spaces between some of your phrases so that in these instances you can devote your full attention to filling out the accompaniment.

TRANSCRIPTION OF TRACK 28

Find the phrase(s) that you've transcribed and check your work.

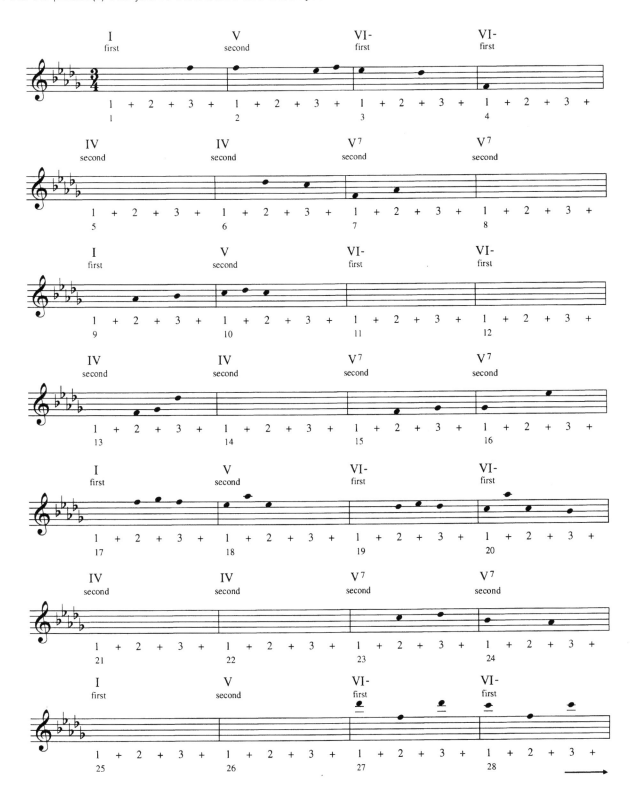

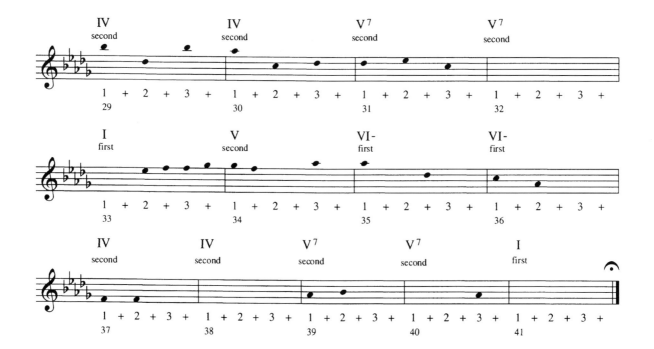

 To benefit further from this transcription, listen to Track 28 and read along. Keep your eyes and ears peeled for examples of the featured improvising techniques. Notice, for example, that both the phrase in measure 13 and the phrase in measures 15-16 begin with the same two notes. Listen to how this use of repetition creates a sense of continuity.

Also notice that the second of these phrases is essentially an expanded version of the first phrase. Specifically, the first phrase has three notes while the second phrase has four; the first phrase features mostly eighth notes while the second phrase features mostly quarter notes; the first phrase ascends to Db while the second phrase extends up another whole step to Eb.

The second phrase can be characterized as a longer, slower, more extended version of the first. Though the phrases are clearly related (creating continuity), the second phrase has expanded into something new (providing variety).

Looking Ahead to Book Two

The music in *Piano by Ear's* Book Two will introduce a new world of melodic, harmonic, and rhythmic possibilities. It will also continue to serve as your guide as you develop your improvising skills through a combination of listening, transcribing, composing, and playing.

Congratulations on completing Book One!

The author, three years old